REPROGRAPHY
for librarians

REPROGRAPHY

for librarians

REPROGRAPHY
for librarians

PETER G NEW

CLIVE BINGLEY LINNET BOOKS
LONDON   HAMDEN · CONN

FIRST PUBLISHED 1975 BY CLIVE BINGLEY LTD
16 PEMBRIDGE ROAD LONDON W11
SIMULTANEOUSLY PUBLISHED IN THE USA BY LINNET BOOKS
AN IMPRINT OF THE SHOE STRING PRESS INC
995 SHERMAN AVENUE HAMDEN CONNECTICUT 06514
IBM SET IN 10 ON 12 POINT JOURNAL ROMAN
PRINTED AND BOUND IN GREAT BRITAIN BY
REDWOOD BURN LTD TROWBRIDGE AND ESHER
COPYRIGHT © PETER G NEW 1975
ALL RIGHTS RESERVED
BINGLEY ISBN: 0-85157-201-4
LINNET ISBN: 0-208-01373-3

Library of Congress Cataloguing in Publication Data

New, Peter.
    Reprography for librarians.

    Includes index.
    1. Copying processes. 2. Microforms. 3. Photo-
copying services in libraries. I. Title.
Z681.N48 1975   686   75-11631
ISBN 0-208-01373-3 (Linnet Books)

CONTENTS

		Page
Preface		7
1	Reprography—what it is	9
2	The basis of choice	17
3	Microcopy—the methods	27
4	Microcopy—uses	41
5	Photocopy	51
6	Multiple reproduction	71
7	Creating the image	87
8	Information sources	97
Index		105

PREFACE

This book, and evidence of the need for it, arises from experience of teaching reprography to students of librarianship for more than fifteen years. There are, of course, many books on reprography, particularly on individual branches such as microcopy and photocopy. But only a handful are oriented towards libraries and of these almost all are confined to parts of the subject or special problems such as catalogue reproduction or photocopying from bound volumes. Only one, to my knowledge, covers the whole subject and this is out of date. My book therefore seeks to fill a gap. It also attempts to provide a new approach.

It is hoped that this brief guide will be found useful to both practising librarian and student. The advanced practitioner in reprography will find nothing new here, but the aim is toward the librarian in the first stages of considering a move into microcopy for example, or thinking of the expansion of his facilities for internally produced reports. Certain areas, such as the uses of microforms in libraries (Chapter IV) are crucial to any librarian, so all students of librarianship might benefit from a quick or selective reading of this volume. Students taking a specialist option in reprography (as at the author's own school of librarianship) may find this useful as a basic text and possibly as a springboard to more detailed study. This last type of user was particularly in mind during the compilation of the book.

To achieve suitability for the readership I have described a deliberate attempt has been made to keep technical detail to a minimum and to concentrate on the principles and general characteristics of the processes. Their advantages, disadvantages and uses are much more important than the intricacies of how they operate or the fine distinctions between one machine and another. Thus no individual push button photocopier is named, for example; instead guidance is given on the range of features by which one could select from the variety of equipment on the market. The reason is not only the aim at simplicity and essentials. Specific information dates rapidly: it would be out of date even before the manuscript reached the printer. In any event the librarian who is at the point of making a choice of equipment to buy would never rely on a textbook, however detailed. He would seek up-to-the-minute data from manufacturers and from independent sources such as the National Reprographic Centre for documentation and the other organisations mentioned in my last chapter.

The same reasoning applies to costs. A warning on the dangers of putting too much trust in detailed cost-per-copy figures in given in Chapter II. And at a time of rapid world wide inflation precise costs of equipment will almost certainly become misleading. There is also the problem of different currencies in a book which may be read in more than one country: it is annoying for the reader to be obliged continually to convert pounds to dollars or *vice versa*. To overcome these difficulties and to give some indication of expense where this is essential I have employed a rough relative method. Thus machine A may be described as half as expensive as machine B, or one process simply as very expensive compared with others. Where it seems necessary to indicate an absolute cost I have hit on the device of comparing with a common article outside reprography—a television set or a car for example. It is hoped that inflation will treat them alike.

My thanks are due to several of my academic colleagues at the Polytechnic of North London who have been asked for advice on some details and to two members of the clerical staff who typed the manuscript and who wish to remain anonymous. I owe a very heavy debt to B J S Williams, Director of the National Reprographic Centre for documentation at Hatfield and his colleague there T Hampshire, Senior Lecturer in Reprography, Hatfield Polytechnic. From these two I have learned much of what I know about reprography, certainly in recent years. In some gesture of gratitude I dedicate this book to them. Tom Hampshire has kindly agreed to read through the script, give advice on Chapter VIII, and help with the illustrations, but of course the responsibility for any errors is mine. Acknowledgement is also made for permission to reproduce photographs to the following; National Reprographic Centre for Documentation (fig 2), Bell and Howell (fig 3), Rank Xerox (figs 4 and 9b), Ozalid (fig 5) and Addressograph-Multigraph (fig 14). Fig 10 is reproduced from Dorothy Harrop *Modern book production,* London, Clive Bingley; Hamden, Conn, Linnet Books, 1968.

P G New
Harpenden
January 1975

CHAPTER I

REPROGRAPHY—WHAT IT IS

Reprography is now the internationally accepted term which replaces the earlier *document copying* or *documentary reproduction*. None of these synonyms is defined in the major general dictionaries, probably because the subject itself is relatively new. More specialised sources give the following:

'*Reprography* The art of producing single or multiple copies of documents, whether by photographic or other means' (Landau, T *ed Encyclopaedia of librarianship* 3rd ed, Bowes and Bowes, 1966).

'Reprography can be defined as the production and reproduction of visual images for business and administrative purposes' (Institute of Reprographic Technology).

Neither of these is wholly satisfactory. They are both too wide (they could apply to printing and computer print out as well as reprography) and the IRT definition seems to exclude libraries.

In any event it is probably not helpful to attempt to encapsulate a somewhat diverse set of techniques with ever expanding applications within a few words. A better understanding may be achieved by setting down the scope of the subject and the major characteristics which are generally applicable throughout. Briefly, reprography includes microcopy, photocopy, duplicating and in-plant printing, and it is in general characterised by the small scale of its operations and the non-professional nature of its operatives.

Characteristics

Such a summary statement requires immediate amplification, and it will be seen that there are exceptions at every turn. The full-time reprographic manager will certainly object to being called non-professional, and rightly so, but his skills are managerial rather than operational. It is broadly true that a wide range of reprographic equipment is deliberately made for use by unskilled staff, or those with very brief training. Push-button electrophotographic office copiers are a clear example. The operator of a small offset machine does not require the years of apprentice-ship demanded of the professional printer. Exceptions to this rule can be found. The old Photostat system, with its large camera and wet photo-graphic processing, required trained photographic technicians, but it is significant that its heyday was before the full evolvement of the modern concept of reprography.

The other general characteristic of reprography—the small scale of operations—can be viewed in two ways. Firstly the finished product is usually restricted to a size smaller than that obtainable by commercial printing. The vast majority of photocopy machines, microform print-outs, duplicators and small offset machines are geared to a maximum of A4 or the old foolscap size. This is in accord with the demand: it would be quite uneconomic for manufacturers to market in many larger sizes. Secondly reprography is small scale in the sense that it is intended to pro-duce relatively few copies of any one item. While this is generally true, the variation between the processes is considerable. At one extreme some photocopy processes are fully economic only when producing one copy of an original; most are suited to very small numbers as is most microcopy. At the other end of the scale small offset can produce the tens of thousands of copies possible in commercial printing: it is more typically used, however, for runs of hundreds rather than thousands.

Scope
We find the same mix of broadly valid concepts and exceptions if we try to define the subjects which make up reprography. Microcopy is fairly clear-cut as it obviously deals in images of a reduced size, almost always requiring some special apparatus to make them readable (the exception is 'micro-litho', low reduction images which can be read with the naked eye). There are few difficulties, either, in drawing the boundaries of photocopy. It is an adaptation of photography whereby copies can be produced directly from originals without the need for re-creation of the image (*eg* by typing) to make a master for subsequent reproduction.

Delineating the exact extent of the subject is not as easy in the over-lapping fields of duplicating and in-plant printing which themselves merge into the domain of the professional printer. Hectographic (spirit or Banda) and wax stencil methods are clearly duplicating and make little attempt to rival printing work in quality or possible length of run. Small offset however is indistinguishable from duplicating at one end of its range and from full scale printing at the other. Offset litho machines are often described by their manufacturers as 'offset duplicators', obviously intended to compete with wax stencil for the same class of work, mainly quickly produced typescript material for internal use. There is no doubt of the success of the campaign, for stencil duplicating is in decline. But the small offset machine is no more and no less than the small brother of the large press operated by commercial printers for high grade work; small litho is technically capable of producing long runs (depending on the plate used) and often very high quality including full colour work.

Although the majority of the use is in the duplicating field, the quality, versatility and volume of work often justifies the more dignified title of in-plant printing, and in the upper reaches, with the use of sophisticated platemaking for tone illustrations and expensive filmsetting equipment for text, the end product cannot be distinguished from that of the professional printer. If a distinction is needed it can normally be made on the basis of the type of organisation undertaking the work; the term 'reprography' might be allowable if the printing operation were non profit making and serving the needs of the larger organisation of which it forms a part. But like many of our definitions it does not hold true in all cases, for there are now many commercially run 'instant print' shops whose class of business is mainly the simple photocopying and duplicating which we would have no hesitation in including within reprography.

Before leaving the scope of the subject it may be as well to correct the impression which may have been given that there is little connection between the three major sections of microcopy, photocopy and duplicating/ in-plant printing. There is a technical connection between them all, namely photography. This is obvious in the case of microcopy and photocopy and appears in small offset in some forms of platemaking. Moreover, specific bridges between the three major techniques can easily be demonstrated. Print out of paper copies from microforms employ some form of photocopy. Plate making for small offset, and less frequently master making for duplicating can be by means of photocopying.

Quality
Perhaps a traditional printer, conservative in outlook, would characterise reprography by its lack of professional quality. His years of training and experience condition him to look at print with a critical eye for perfection in typography and presswork. He would dismiss reprography as not up to his standards in these respects, and what is more, often incapable of justifying the lines of text, part of the printer's mystique. (In fact, as we shall see in Chapter VII, justification is an unnecessary historical hangover). It was this contemptuous attitude which led printers to lose much business

to in-plant installations, until, on the principle of 'if you can't beat 'em, join 'em', some printing houses began to install small offset equipment, and the growth of profit-making 'instant print' shops was boosted.

The truth of the matter is that one can be over concerned with quality. With the growing professionalism of reprography we now find reprographers themselves being over-pernickety; they peer at a perfectly acceptable image through a magnifier and tut-tut at a slightly unsharp or broken comma. In an effort to prove that he is as good as any printer the reprographer is therefore in danger of falling into the same trap of pursuing the highest quality for its own sake.

Microcopy can be excluded at once from this consideration because the inevitable image loss in the reduction and subsequent enlargement involved demands high standards. But even here there is a difference between the stringent requirements of the 150—times reduced PCMI microfiche and what will serve for a public library loans record on 16mm film. Elsewhere in reprography the highest quality possible is justified when there is a direct competition with professional print, where there is a need to impress the recipient, or indeed to demonstrate to some highly placed decision maker that reprography is capable of a wider range of work than he thinks.

But high quality often means extra money: and further expenditure may not be warranted. The extra cost may come from the greater care needed for a perfect job—the longer time involved (which raises labour costs), and the scrapping of imperfect attempts. Or it may come from the investment in more expensive equipment—'justifying' typewriters to give an even right-hand edge to the page for example. So for many applications something less than the ultimate is in order. There is no reason why internal memoranda should not be reproduced by spirit duplicating which does not claim the highest quality image, and if a photocopy with a few smudges is allowable, the doubled cost of doing the job again is avoided.

Fortunately, modern reprography enables acceptable to high quality to be achieved at modest cost particularly if the problems presented by the original to be reproduced are limited (*eg* no colours or no tone illus-trations). A modern electrophotographic machine shows its superiority in quality over the early thermographic copiers, and in consistency over the photographic transfer methods (thus avoiding the expense of their wastage). Only at the upper reaches of reprography, where, at the borders of professional printing, problems such as full-colour tone illustrations are tackled must the highest standards be met by considerable expense. But the mass of reprographic work does not lie here, and it is unfair to judge the whole by untypical parts.

Growth: copyright
The origins of reprography could be traced back for a surprising distance into history: an example is the first use of microcopy in the nineteenth century. There would, however, be little profit in this exercise: reprography as we now know it is a recent phenomenon. The rapid and accelerating growth of the subject stems from the 1950s and particularly the 1960s.

This book is concerned with the implications of reprography for libraries, but it must be emphasised that the impetus for the development of the techniques came largely from industry, business and government. Libraries therefore form a small part of the market for reprographic equipment. There are large areas of reprographic activity of no interest to libraries such as the reproduction of engineering drawings by photocopy and microcopy, and business systems employing all the techniques. Moreover the general copying equipment is naturally designed with the majority user in mind, so that library users are rarely specifically catered for. It is true that libraries can usually meet their needs from the wide range of machines currently available, but it is as well to draw attention to the potential danger if a library has a special need. To exemplify from the past:— when some early photocopy systems appeared on the market they were frequently in 'rotary' form, *ie* they would take single sheets, but not books. Rotaries were cheaper, more efficient, and suited office use—libraries could not use the method until the more expensive book copiers were developed. Similarly, photographic book issue systems in public libraries still use standard 16mm cameras or adaptations intended for the recording of cheques or credit cards. An up-to-date example of a library need not being met is the occasional necessity to produce a second copy of a card catalogue. There is no doubt that it is technically possible to devise a relatively simple electrophotographic machine to be fed with cards in sequence and to output a duplicate sequence on properly sized and punched 5ins x 3ins cards, but it is equally certain that it is uneconomic for a manufacturer to tool up for such a limited market.

There is then, whether or not designed for library use, a vast range of reprographic equipment available today, capable of reproducing almost anything. The enormous number of copies being made poses problems for users. Librarians, in particular, are aware of this aspect of the 'paper explosion': apart from the major consideration of copyright, more minor worries include questions of handling, storage, permanence of copies, and methods of information retrieval. Is it worth indexing, cataloguing or classifying a cheap photocopy or microfiche received, and if so, how? These queries must be left to the librarian to resolve in the context of his own reader needs.

A major and general problem is that of copyright. No attempt will be made here to give the detailed provisions of copyright regulations: they are available elsewhere (see Mason's book cited in Chapter VIII). The minutiae are very difficult to memorise and tend to obscure rather than clarify the main principles involved. Also some of the terms used in Britain such as 'a substantial part' or 'a reasonable proportion' are ill-defined and have never been tested in a court of law, although legal battles rage in other countries. And as will be seen the theory does not accord with practice. The underlying principle is that authors and publishers depend for a return on their work on the sale of copies; reprographic methods can easily reproduce multiple copies from a single original and can therefore decrease seriously the sales of the commercially produced originals. Copyright acts and regulations seek to restrict unreasonably large scale copying of material still in copyright, while allowing some restricted amount of copying to take place under certain conditions.

The reality is that illicit copying is widespread. It could hardly be otherwise when the potential to multiply copies is so readily to hand and when the motives of convenience and economy combine with the virtual unenforceability of the restrictions. Even if top administrators and reprographic managers do everything they can to secure compliance with the law, there is little hope that all those who use freely available push-button copiers will do so. In the tangled copyright situation there are therefore two reasonably held but conflicting points of view. The special library which photocopies multiple copies of large sections of a new periodical to give to interested readers is acting illegally on more than one count, but is, under its own lights, properly pursuing its policy of dissemination of information. On the other hand the periodical publisher can justly claim that he has lost the sales of the multiple copies which the library should have bought.

With universal disregard of unenforceable restrictions the time is over-ripe for a fundamental rethinking of the concept of copyright and its applicability to copying. Simply to allow a free-for-all in copying would condone and increase the damage to authors and publishers. Per-haps we must now recognise, as B J S Williams suggests (see reference in Chapter VIII) that the multiplication of texts is nowadays not confined to the publisher/printer combination: it is also taking place lower down the information chain nearer the point of use, eg by libraries, information centres, and the user himself. To reconcile freedom to copy with a proper return to the author and publisher, some fee for copying seems needed. Problems of recording of copies made, distribution of the proceeds, and distinguishing between copyright and non-copyright material would have to be tackled.

The involvement of the librarian
The growth of reprography and its recognition as a subject of study have prompted the formulation of bodies such as the Institute of Reprographic Technology which awards qualifications to its members. This emergence of a profession also arises from the appointment of capable and senior personnel to posts of Manager of Reprographic Services and the like. The growing professionalism in reprography and its use of an ever widening range of sometimes expensive equipment encourages the trend towards centralised reprographic units within organisations.

In view of this trend the extent to which the professional librarian has, or should have, an interest in reprography may be questioned. The question is particularly germane now that education for librarianship no longer requires the student to master details of law, architecture and furniture as they may apply to libraries, on the sensible principle that there are experts to call upon if needed. The same principle does apply to some extent to reprography, but there are few experts to call upon who can apply reprography to librarianship. So it is not unreasonable that some librarians should be fairly well acquainted with the subject, particularly if they have special reprographic techniques under their control in their libraries. This is paralleled by the situation in the computer world: here again there is a body of librarians building up an expertise in the field because of its application to their library problems. No-one is suggesting, in computers or in reprography, that *all* librarians need a high level of detailed information; all would benefit, however, from some general awareness of the use that can be made of the techniques.

There is no need to labour the case for the involvement of librarians with microtechniques: the obvious and immense benefits to librarians which come from microrecording, microstorage and micropublishing are such that they call for a whole chapter of this book (Chapter IV). But as is frequently the case with microcopy, it stands apart, self contained, from the other techniques. For reprography generally it may be said that the librarian's involvement may be either administrative or, in the wide sense, bibliographic. Administratively, the librarian or information officer may be in charge of a reprographic unit or closely associated with it: it is not uncommon in special libraries for the librarian to be responsible for the production of technical reports. Clearly the librarian in this situation must be aware of the pro and con of equipment available for purchase, and must make reasoned decisions on which process is suitable for a particular job.

The bibliographic, or reader services, implications of reprography for librarians parallel those set out in detail in Chapter IV on microforms. In brief the librarian is serving his readers whether by acquiring material for them in a non-conventional form—perhaps a photocopy, or an unpublished report produced by small offset—or by creating materials by reprographic means, *eg* booklists, literature searches, guides to the use of the library, etc. In both aspects he is helped by some knowledge of the processes used to make the materials he is handling.

This leads to a wider statement which justifies the librarian's study of reprography to an appropriate depth. Any true profession has as its concern a body of knowledge wider than that which is strictly required for the operation of day to day activities. Thus the history of libraries is quite rightly studied although it would be difficult to prove frequent instances of direct practical usefulness. A much closer comparison is with the subject of modern book production—widely studied by librarianship students, either in outline or as a specialist option. Here there is certainly some practical value in assisting the librarian's decisions on rebinding, for example, but this is not the major justification for studying the subject. The fundamental justification is that librarians' business is the transfer of information and they therefore reasonably have an interest in the vehicle in which the transfer takes place. If this is true of book production it is equally true of the newer systems of information transfer which are coming to the fore. The traditional codex form of book is not in decline, but a share of the ever increasing mass of recorded information is being handled by other media—computers, sound tapes, films, and in our field micro and other copies. The very novelty of the new forms makes it particularly important that librarians are familiar with them.

CHAPTER II

THE BASIS OF CHOICE

The librarian, in the highly technical world of reprography, often finds himself an uninformed layman. The same is true of data processing and sophisticated equipment generally. Other chapters of this book seek to remedy that deficiency in the various branches of reprography, but there is room for a general consideration of the factors which would be taken into account in choosing one reprographic method rather than another. These factors may be employed when deciding on equipment to buy for a reprographic unit, or in choosing which method to use for a particular job, from the range of processes already installed.

The uninformed librarian is at the mercy of the salesman. Sales representatives of reputable companies are brimming with technical knowledge and can fully explain their product to well briefed customers without undue puffing. At this level no wool is pulled over anyone's eyes. At the other end of the scale, a salesman, undoubtedly human and almost certainly being paid on a commission basis, probably exaggerates the advantages of the gleaming machine he has to sell, and fails to mention the drawbacks, or at least, soft-pedals them. The safeguard is for the customer—the librarian—to be knowledgeable enough to have a set of searching questions to ask.

Perhaps a special word of warning is needed on 'bargain offers'. Some, of course, are quite genuine, but the pressure on salesmen to make a sale can lead to dubious if not sharp practice. Some years ago the author was offered, at nearly half price, a photocopier described as a 'shop soiled ex-demonstration machine'. The salesman, from a large international company prominent in reprography, failed to mention that this model was about to be discontinued. The machine was not satisfactory and maintenance men were frequently called in. On each visit they expressed greater and greater surprise at the antiquity of our model and increased the pressure to buy a more up-to-date machine (which would have been totally unsuited to our needs). My only redress was to warn my students of this company by name. By now some two thousand potential buyers will have received the message.

A demonstration of the equipment should be seen before any decision to install is made. It is far better in most circumstances to have the demonstration at the library or unit where the process will be employed. In some cases an 'on approval' period can be arranged. At the library the machine may be tested on the kind of work it will do during its lifetime: there may be snags not otherwise apparent. Here too the staff involved in operating the machine and using its products may have their say: too often the 'top man', responsible for the buying decision, is out of touch with the practicalities. There are dangers in accepting without further checks the evidence from a demonstration in the manufacturer's showroom or a trade exhibition. So often an amazing photocopy or a superb piece of four-colour printing is pressed into one's hands at an exhibition: the quality is such that it can rarely be repeated in normal working conditions. This 'exhibition syndrome' may be caused by having machines highly tuned and maintained beyond normal practicability; possibly by using better than usual materials, papers etc; and by allowing the machine to take the credit for a high quality original or piece of ancillary equipment. (Thus the excellence of full colour offset work may depend largely on expensive sophisticated colour separation and platemaking). Exhibitions, too, tend to show the latest and most advanced techniques which can be a disadvantage. Sometimes the exhibition model is from abroad, and is not available on the home market (colour photocopiers for example), sometimes a much vaunted process fails to become important and soon drops out of the scene, as exemplified by Adherography, and, earlier, multicopy transfer copiers.

Running costs
'Cost per copy' is a strong weapon in the salesman's armoury, and much effort is expended by reprographers on this statistic. Certainly on the face of it this appears to be a most important tool in making a case for or against purchase of equipment or use of a particular process. Clearly in all applications of reprography as in other ventures the maximum must be gained for the least cost, and the air of precision which cost per copy calculations give lends an authenticity to any argument.

But cost per copy is so often a snare and a delusion. At the very best figures must be fully understood and used with the greatest care; indeed they often require a costing expert to interpret them. Moreover cost per copy is not in practice an over-riding factor in the choice of process. Particularly when the difference in costs between one method and another is marginal (but not only then) other considerations may be far more important: the convenience and speed of use: the quality aimed at: the limitations imposed by the kind of work to be done. In practice too the reprographer must use for any job a process from the range he has available. It is perfectly reasonable in many circumstances to use a strictly 'uneconomic' method for the sake of internal control and speed, rather than buy special equipment or put the job outside.

Figures for cost per copy are so often deceptive because the basis on which any particular costing is compiled is frequently unknown or misunderstood. Perhaps, too, the costing itself is imperfect, ignoring factors which the user assumes to be included. The simplest system confines itself to the cost of the expendable materials: thus if a small offset master costs x, 1000 sheets of paper y, and the ink used on this quantity z, the cost per copy on a 'cost of materials' basis is obviously

$$\frac{x + y + z}{1000}.$$

While clear-cut, this type of costing is of limited value until we add other considerations, and now the calculation becomes much more complicated and liable to be less certain. The initial cost of the machine can be amortised, although sometimes it is on another budget or shared by another department. The electric power to run the machines is a factor in exact calculations. Labour rates will vary widely in different employment situations and in different types of library (Do reprographic operatives run the machines or are they for intermittent use by library staff, sometimes relatively highly paid?) The whole area of overheads is difficult to calculate and can easily be overlooked—the cost of the space the machine takes up, and a proportion of the administrative and managerial expense of the reprographic service.

Two factors in costing deserve a special mention. The first is the important problem of wastage. A machine which produces more than the inevitable minimum of unusable copies wastes not only materials but staff time (and therefore money) in putting the error right. Notorious examples can be found from the old 'peel-apart' transfer methods of photocopying. Here an error in exposure (and some experience was necessary for good results) or cockling of the face-to-face sheets emerging from the machine could waste a copy. A second or third attempt to get it right would double or treble the cost per usable copy, thus making nonsense of the careful costing figures in the textbook or the manufacturer's brochure.

The second special factor, often ignored, and virtually impossible for the costing specialist to evaluate, is the cost of *not* installing the machine or using the process in question. Frequently this cannot be expressed in financial terms but the efficiency of the library as an information centre may be impaired. This is no more than saying that while a watchful eye must always be kept on costs, the needs of the central purpose of the library—its service to readers—must be paramount. It may be dubious, on a strictly costing basis, to supply microform readers so liberally that they can be taken home for long periods, but such a policy could be repaid a thousandfold in some breakthrough in scholarship or research.

For most purposes this over-concentration on cost per copy can be replaced by something less precise but more usable, namely a knowledge of the approximate range, in terms of numbers of copies, for which each process is economic. Strictly speaking this alternative should also be based on nice calculations, but a rough idea will be of some help. The old photographic transfer processes, for example, became wildly uneconomic at a very small number of copies from one original, but despite the fact that other, cheaper methods were available, they were still in ignorance used for multiple copying. This sort of vague guide to costing will suffice for many users, bearing in mind the other, non-financial factors in choice. And at least the student is spared the useless chore of memorising exact cost per copy figures which may be unsound, misunderstood, and ever subject to change.

Initial costs
The purchase price of reprographic equipment ranges from the insignificant through current expenditure items to major capital expenditure schemes. It is axiomatic that highly expensive machines can only be justified if they are heavily used. Even allowing for the non-financial factors many libraries will find some processes beyond any reasonable level of expenditure unless they can find some alternative to outright purchase of an item perhaps only intermittently used. Luckily such alternatives exist.

The field of microfilming provides many examples of using facilities on a bureau or service basis whereby a fee is paid to a commercial organisation to do the work. Thus no capital expenditure is involved, and while the payment naturally includes profit margins and is more expensive than using owned equipment if it were justified, costs are restricted to the work done, and a fully professional result may be expected. Libraries can have all their microfilming done for them, or they may have their own cameras and put the processing outside. The very high cost of recorders for COM (computer output on microfilm) means that in almost all cases libraries with a computer generated catalogue will have this work done by a COM bureau. Plate making for full colour small offset work is another area in which if the need is only occasional the purchase of the equipment and the build-up of the necessary expertise is not justified.

Many libraries were able to install a new sophisticated form of photocopying well beyond their capital resources by the introduction of the rental system by Xerox in the 1960's. Rental has great advantages beyond facilitating payment from current expenditure. It is possible always to have an up-to-date machine: if a new model appears which better suits the library's needs no loss is incurred in abandoning the old. Maintenance is part of the rental agreement and is usually prompt. Rental can, however, be overdone. It is not unknown for some manufacturers to hire out machines at an incredibly low rental—seemingly uneconomic for them—only to take their profit on the expensive photocopy paper which the hirer is obliged to use. Rental started because electrophotographic copiers were too expensive for widespread purchase but nowadays some simple copiers using this system are available for outright sale at a modest cost. With a fair degree of use and a maintenance contract, these could be economic propositions.

The full cost of purchase—or of rental—may be avoided by sharing the use of machines with other departments of the library's parent organisation where this is appropriate. One electrophotographic copier may be sufficient to serve the needs not only of a small special library but the head office administration of the body of which it forms a part. Readers, too, can share the cost of providing machines by means of the coin-operation facility available on some. But reader payment should be decided by library policy rather than forced by economic need.

Quality of copy required
Some general comments on quality in reprography were given in Chapter I. Here we may assume that sensible decisions are being made on the balance between cost, type of use, and the standard expected for a particular job. Nevertheless the choice of a process will depend heavily on the quality of work of which it is capable.

'Poor quality' often means the unsharp image which is characteristic, for example, of hectrographic duplicating or the original Thermofax method of photocopying. It may also mean the unpleasant paper found in stencil duplicating and the coated paper variant of electrophotographic copying. Of course it is easy to achieve bad results in methods which are not inherently low in quality: poor platemaking and presswork can make a sorry, spotty mess of small offset.

There is, however, no problem in finding a suitable process to give high quality, whether duplicating or photocopy, if the requirement is merely to reproduce text and line illustrations. Fewer processes can manage tone illustrations successfully. This is true of photocopy, untrue of microforms, and true of duplicating and small offset unless the expense of screens and plate makers is incurred. Copies in colour are even more difficult to achieve. Apart from the possibility of different overall colours in dyeline, the colour photocopier is only just arriving on the scene although it has been heralded for some time. It is doubtful if there will be a big market for it at the price which it is necessary to charge. Microcopy, being purely photographic, can give excellent colours, but at a price, while duplicating can manage multi colours in line work. Small offset, when it nudges the boundary with professional printing, can produce full colour work, but again, as always, at some multiplication of the cost of simpler work.

Type of original to be copied
It is unlikely that anyone would be so ill informed as to purchase a machine which was incapable of tackling the kind of work most commonly required in the library or information unit concerned. But issues are rarely as clear cut as this: sometimes it is useful if equipment can serve two kinds of copying need: sometimes versatility is assumed at the point of purchase, but when installed the machine will not undertake everything that was hoped for. Apart from these initial purchase problems, the type of original influences the process chosen for a particular job from the range of equipment already installed.

A fundamental choice is between photocopying and duplicating or small offset. We may ignore cost and other factors as they are dealt with separately, but may observe in passing that for substantial numbers photocopy must be more expensive. The influence of type of original may be demonstrated by somewhat extreme examples. If the original to be copied is visually acceptable as it stands (a type set periodical article for example) the bias is towards photocopy. If it is unacceptable (material written in blunt pencil on the backs of old brown envelopes) then obviously it must be retyped, and it is sensible to type directly on to an offset or duplicating master rather than on to a sheet of paper for subsequent photocopy. But retyping should be avoided wherever possible: it is a sound principle of reprography that once an acceptable image has been created it should be reproduced without the need for recreation at any stage. Retyping is not only expensive in typist's time (often much more expensive than the reproduction cost) but it necessitates rechecking for errors, usually by a relatively highly paid person. Therefore even if length of run leads to the choice of duplicating or small offset, photocopying of an acceptable original is far better as a master making method than direct typing.

Retyping and master making in a sense recreates the originals in a form compatible to the reproduction method chosen. Photocopying does not need to recreate—it uses 'uncontrolled' originals and therefore it is not surprising that some kinds of work are unsuited to some kinds of copying process. The dyeline method for example employs a 'direct' method of exposure, transmitting light through the original. While this is eminently suitable for dyeline's major application of engineering drawings, the process is totally unsuited to books or any other type of two sided original, so is little used in libraries. In any photocopy process libraries will require a flat-bed book copier: the cheaper, neater and sometimes more efficient rotary copiers are intended for single papers, having merely a slot for the receipt of the originals. Fortunately, most modern electrophotographic copiers are flat bed, but earlier processes were often first introduced in rotary form (demonstrating that the office market is more important than libraries to manufacturers—see p13). Tightly bound books can be damaged from the pressure needed to achieve close contact: valuable books may therefore call for avoidance of contact photocopying altogether and a reliance on microcopy and other camera methods. Finally, originals in colour limit the number of suitable photocopy methods available. It is notorious that the thermographic processes copy only metallic or carbon inks; vegetable dyes used for coloured inks do not reproduce at all. Some other methods do not distinguish between colours so that for example a red heading on a green rectangle would be reproduced by an unreadable uniform black.

Speed and convenience of use

In long run work, especially where machines are in constant use, the running speed of a machine is important. Just as in conventional printing a high rate of copies per hour is an important aspect of productivity. The reprographic situation most closely akin to professional printing—long run small offset in a large in-plant department—will naturally look for high speed machines for this reason.

But a very great deal of reprography is short run and intermittent work. This is undoubtedly true of microcopy and most photocopy, and much duplicating and small offset is used for a modest number of copies, and the machine is not running all day. In these situations the speed at which the wheels revolve in the machine is not important; a speed of thousands of copies an hour is of no significance if only six copies are wanted. Much more relevant is the time taken to set up the machine ready to copy, or the speed and convenience of changing from copying one original to copying the next. Some special versions of small offset machines offer quick change of masters, and electrophotographic copiers have eliminated the preparation of chemicals needed to start photocopying. Indeed the latter inconvenience often meant that if the use of machines was only occasional, it was better to do copying in batches rather than undertake the chore of preparation (even if only pouring out developer) for a single copy.

Speed and convenience are therefore interrelated; the inconvenient process is likely to be slow or infrequently used. But caution is needed in condemning a whole process: sometimes clever design of individual machines can overcome what appears to be an inherent drawback. For example, photocopy systems using chemical developers may be dismissed as messy because of the risk of spillage and the chore of filling and emptying developing trays fairly frequently to avoid the encrustation and smell of oxidising chemicals. But some clever manufacturers have incorporated a plastic sachet which releases developer to the place wanted on switching on and withdraws it on switching off. So mess, smell and handling is avoided. Linked switches and other ingenious control devices can make other processes—like the inherently complex lithography—simple to use.

Finally, and obviously, safety and accommodation factors need a mention. While much reprographic equipment is deliberately compact to make it suitable for office use, clearly a full scale in-plant printing installation or a complete microfilming unit demand special space set aside for them. The ammonia fumes in the dyeline process must be ducted away to the outside air, so limitations may be imposed on the position of the machine.

Skill in use: staffing

It was suggested in Chapter I that one of the major characteristics of reprography is the lack of formal training required of its operatives. Thus even when small-offset work rivals that of commercial printers it is most unlikely that those producing the work have had any considerable training—certainly nothing approaching the years of apprenticeship called for by the printing industry. It is true that photographic technicians may be employed in the processing of microfilm and to operate the old Photostat cameras, but on the other hand much photocopy is now push-button and duplicating a simple office technique.

Generalising over the whole field of reprography it would of course be wrong to say that no skills are required: the point being made is that formal training courses and qualifications are rarely needed. The requisite skills are largely picked up on the job, imparted by more senior staff, or in some cases a short training period is arranged by the manufacturer of the equipment. This could range from a simple demonstration when the machine is installed to a short course at the company's training centre.

It might be thought from this argument that reprographic machines might be used by anyone within the organisation as required. Some processes, for example push-button electrophotographic photocopiers, seem designed for this, but even here there is need for some caution and control. It is a sound general rule that use, or at least responsibility for, equipment should be in the hands of as few people as possible. Where the amount of reprographic work in a library justifies full time staff for this purpose alone they should be appointed. This is cheaper and more efficient than using library staff. Where such special full-time appointments are not justified, one of the exisiting staff should be given special responsibility for reprographic work. This need not preclude use by others of the simplest equipment and arrangements for emergencies. Many libraries and information units will find that reprography, or at least some parts of it such as in-plant printing, is centralised within their parent organisation and serves other departments as well as their own. In many respects this is efficient as it groups together staff expertise and facilitates the employment of expensive equipment not otherwise justified. But rapid access to the reprographic service must be ensured and some simple copying could be decentralised to the point of use.

The value of using specialist operators (experienced, not necessarily formally trained) will be readily appreciated by anyone who has suffered from equipment put out of action by mis-handling. ('I thought the lever went that way . . .') Even the best machines can jam if the paper is not properly prepared before insertion. Apart from the disruption caused by machine downtime, inexperienced use can cause heavy waste of materials. Exposure on some photocopy processes may be critical, or the handling may require some knack, so that unless some expertise has been built up it is probable that many useless copies are produced before one that is usable. Furthermore someone designated to be in charge of the machine will keep a check on its general state of health and supplies of materials; no-one cares in a 'free for all' situation and supplies or machine may fail at a critical time. In short, the policy of giving special responsibility to certain staff for reprographic equipment itself fosters in those concerned an attitude of 'responsibility' and brings with it increased efficiency.

Permanence

This factor in the choice of a process is left until last because it is not important in much reprographic work. A large amount of the output of reprographic units is ephemeral in content. Also the problem now arises much less frequently than in the past: modern electrophotographic copiers give a stable carbon image. Small offset and stencil duplicating are permanent. With microcopy permanent unless storage or processing is at fault, the problem of impermanence is confined to lesser processes.

Hectographic duplicating, for example, fades on exposure to strong sunlight. This is a reason why some do not favour it for library catalogues, (although one rarely sees a catalogue in full sun). It used to be said that photocopy paid for its speed, convenience and cheapness by lack of permanence, but this is disproved by the current methods available. Certainly the semi-dry quickly stabilized photographic processes could discolour badly unless the residual chemicals were washed out, which would take away the speed and convenience. The Thermofax heat copying method needs no development at all, and so the copies remain sensitive to heat, eventually blackening if exposed to the heat of the sun. On the one hand it is claimed that the lack of fixing enables copies to be amended and updated: but on the other hand this presents a serious security drawback in some applications.

CHAPTER III

MICROCOPY—THE METHODS

We have used the term 'microcopy' in the chapter heading above as it is generally familiar in libraries. So are 'microtexts' and 'microforms' which are used here and in the next chapter interchangeably to save constant repetition of the same word. Some experts now prefer to speak of 'micrographics'. While 'microtext' strictly construed would exclude illustrations, 'graphics' is often taken to mean non-text design. Whichever word is used, both text and illustration are intended unless otherwise specified.

Before examining each of the different formats of micro material, a prefatory note is needed on colour microfilm; thereafter in this chapter black and white will be assumed, as it forms the overwhelming majority of all types of microtext. Obviously colour is far more expensive than black and white—perhaps seven or eight times as much. A comparison of the costs of amateur snapshot film will show this. But in some applications colour is vital, for example in the microfilming of an illuminated manuscript. (Incidentally, colour microfilms are technically indistinguishable from filmstrips, now almost always produced in colour). Much material microfilmed, however, has only the occasional need of a colour frame, and the decision has to be made whether to shoot all on expensive colour film, or to use black and white and sacrifice the benefit of reproducing colour in the one or two frames requiring it.

Reel microfilm

It is appropriate to start with the oldest established of the microforms but not only for historical reasons; reel microfilm remains a most important technique. Of the various widths of photographic film available, only 35mm and 16mm need concern us in the library use context. Of these the originally predominant 35mm format is retained largely because of its usefulness in recording large originals such as newspapers. The main development effort has been directed to 16mm because of its cheaper film and equipment costs and because of the big market for business systems. Most of the references in this chapter to microfilm refer to 16mm therefore and are not necessarily true of 35mm.

The standard length of film is 100 feet or 30 metres, giving over 2000 pictures or 'frames' in 16mm, about 800 in 35mm. These rough figures depend on the shape of the original and the ratio of reduction. (Over 20 times reduction in the case of 16mm; 12-18 times for 35mm. Reduction ratios are expressed as 20X). The number of frames quoted also presupposes only one frame across the width of the film. This is the commonest form of filming, certainly for libraries, and is termed 'simplex' to distinguish from 'duplex' and 'duo' techniques. Some cameras are able to photograph both sides of a single sheet document (not a book) simultaneously: the images appear side by side on the film. This is 'duplex' filming. In 'duo' filming only one half of the width of the film is initially used to record images: the film is then turned round rather like 8mm amateur movie film, and images made on the other half. Thus the final film has two rows of frames as in duplex, but the two sequences are quite separate in the way that twin tracks on magnetic tape have no relationship to each other.

Of much more significance is the orientation of the image on the film. The two possibilities are amusingly but quite officially termed *ciné* and *comic* mode. Ciné derives from the way the frames are arranged in movie film, comic presumably gets its name from the strip cartoons. In comic the text runs parallel to the length of the film, in ciné across it. The choice between the two is determined by the shape of the original and the reduction ratio required, for example a single newspaper page would suffer the least reduction, and therefore be likely to be of maximum readability, in ciné mode on unperforated 35mm film. (The absence of sprocket holes in the margins allows for a larger size image). Obviously the two modes should not be mixed in one piece of filming if constant swivelling of the head, or of the reading equipment (if possible) is to be avoided when viewing the finished film. Ciné mode has a distinct advantage over comic, particularly if rapid-wind microfilm readers are used. A stop between frames in comic mode would show on the screen two part pages with no line of text complete: no reading is possible until the frame is centred. But in ciné mode the two part pages would have their lines complete and so could be read. (See Diagram 1). Indeed this advantage can be taken further. If filming is done from previously printed material, the page layout is naturally fixed, but if the text is produced solely for microfilming, page divisions may be dispensed with, appreciably increasing the capacity of the film. Thus we have the interesting prospect

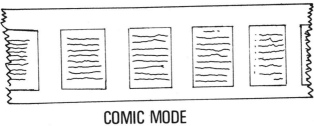

COMIC MODE

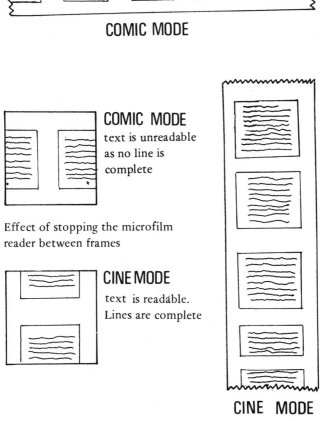

COMIC MODE
text is unreadable
as no line is
complete

Effect of stopping the microfilm
reader between frames

CINE MODE
text is readable.
Lines are complete

CINE MODE

Fig 1: Orientation of images on microfilm

of a departure from the traditional page form, which has been the necessary adjunct of the codex form of book for nearly two thousand years. In effect page-less ciné mode is a return to the scroll form.

For many years microfilm, like sound recording magnetic tape, was available only in open-reel form. The end had to be threaded into the reading machine before use; not a difficult operation, but fiddly and time consuming, and liable to lead to damage in inexperienced hands. Now, as with tape recordings, cartridges and cassettes are available to simplify machine loading and to provide a convenient form of film storage. A cartridge has one reel, so the film must be rewound into it before removal from the reader; a cassette, having two reels, may be loaded or unloaded without rewinding. Unfortunately the rival makes are not compatible, so a certain brand of cassette can only be used on the range of machines of one manufacturer. This contrasts with the sensible standardisation in tape recording cassettes. An encouraging new development however is the cassette which can be loaded with two standard sized microfilm reels.

Unitised microfilm: microfiche
Microfilm is widely used for recording long runs of material but it suffers from the inherent drawback of the 30 metre length. This is the difficulty of 'findability' and 'filability' of individual items. A year's issues of a periodical presents the minimum problem—there is a natural sequence to help in finding the way through the film. But a series of separate reports would need an index and numbered frames with perhaps one of the more sophisticated finding devices referred to below. (*Cameras and reading machines: information retrieval*).

Unitised microfilm and microfiche offer ways of overcoming the findability/filability problem. At its simplest unitised microfilm is merely cutting up microfilm into conveniently sized strips—say eight to ten frames, or the length of a periodical article—and filing the strips in envelopes bearing full size identification details. A special form of unitised microfilm is the aperture card, a standard data processing punched card with one frame of 35mm microfilm inserted. This frame can contain one image, as widely used for engineering drawings, or can be '8-up' as for patents. There is here the potential for an information retrieval system, albeit crude and slow. The other methods of unitised microfilm merge into microfiche. Transparent jackets can be obtained into which strips of 16mm or 35mm film can be inserted in rows: this technique incorporates the facility of updating and is used for hospital

Fig 2a: Microforms—open reel, aperture cards, micro-opaques and microfiches

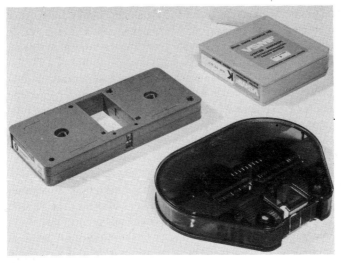

Fig 2 b: Cartridges and cassettes

case records. In another system rows of 16mm film are attached by a thin strip of adhesive on the edges to a base film sheet. Both of these methods could be described as do-it-yourself microfiches.

The microfiche proper is a rectangle of film containing images in rows and with an eye-legible heading. It can be made by a special 'step and repeat' camera (see below under *Filming and reading equipment*) or more simply can be a copy of an original produced by one of the 'do it yourself' methods described at the end of the last paragraph. Fiches can come in various sizes but most are now of A6 size and contain either 60 or 98 frames at 20X or 24X. (British Standard BS4187: 1973 or International Standard ISO 2707). These commonly used forms are known as standard microfiche and could be readily made by a library with its own microfilming unit. This is in contrast to the recently introduced high-reduction microfiches which are publishing ventures only. *Superfiche* has a 75X reduction and can accommodate 1000 pages on one fiche; *ultrafiche*, made by the PCMI process of National Cash Register, contains 3200 pages per fiche at a reduction of 150:1. There is no doubt that microfiche is now the dominant microform, particularly for library applications. Problems of findability and filability are minimised, and the capacity of a fiche is suitable for many kinds of material. A standard fiche will take a technical report; a full book may be accommodated on one to four fiches depending on its length and the kind of fiche chosen. (Indeed superfiche and ultrafiche will take many books!). Moreover standard fiches are cheap to make, and very convenient and cheap to duplicate. The obvious benefits in dissemination of information will be explored in Chapter IV.

As they employ photographic chemistry, microfiches are produced first in negative form from which positive copies can be made. The same is true of other microforms, but in the case of fiche which is so cheap and easy to produce, the necessity of making a positive copy (so making the process a two-stage one) may be questioned. In most cases there is no need to make a positive, unless copies are required in any event. Some people prefer to read a negative as there is less glare on the reader screen— all that is illuminated is the image, against a restful black background. This applies to text and line illustration, but obviously tone illustrations will be meaningless in negative so a positive copy is needed here. There are three ways of making a duplicate. The diazo process is cheapest, but does not reverse the tones, so that a negative is duplicated as a negative (but by the same token a positive original is not made into a negative copy). The vesicular method (trade name Kalvar) which forms its image of minute gas bubbles is a little more expensive, but does change negative to positive and vice versa. The normal photographic silver halide process, by which the original fiche was made, can also be used. It gives the greatest assurance of permanence (in contrast to diazo), it changes tone from negative to positive, but is the slowest and most expensive of the methods.

Micro-opaque
If microfiche is in the ascendant, micro-opaque is (with a few exceptions) in decline. Opaques vary in size from 5ins x 3ins to 6ins x 9ins but they may be thought of as the equivalent of microfiches on card instead of film, and it is largely this essential difference which has brought about their downfall. They are publishing rather than library methods and a card cannot be easily and cheaply duplicated like a microfiche. Also since viewing equipment must depend on reflected, not transmitted light as in the transparent microforms, it is less efficient. This means that a micro-opaque viewer will either give a less good image than a transparency reader or it is much more powerful and therefore expensive. For this reason it is difficult to get a satisfactory print out of a full size copy from a reader printer machine, few of which exist. Another reason for the decline of opaques is economic: they are not as cheap as microfiche in small numbers. While a single microfiche is an economic proposition, a fiche must be made as an intermediary stage in producing an opaque.

The term 'microcard' has so far been avoided deliberately. It is commonly used of 5ins x 3ins micro-opaques but it is a trade name and should strictly be applied to products of Microcard Editions which have a rigidly controlled layout. These and many other micro-opaques are produced in a conventional photographic manner, *ie* they are positive bromide prints from a negative (a negative fiche in fact). The exception is the long established Readex Microprint which is a 6ins x 9ins card printed photolithographically. Thus although photo reduction is used in making the negative, the finished image is made by printer's ink, not silver chemicals on photographic bromide paper. So the economics of printing rather than those of microcopy apply; a sufficiently large edition must be assured to keep the price per copy down.

The one section of micro-opaques which is not dying is akin to Readex Microprint in that it is lithographically printed and therefore requires an edition of some size to make it pay. This is 'micro-litho' or 'miniaturised print'. The distinction of this method is that the reduction ratio is very low (perhaps only 2X) and it is intended to be read with the naked eye or with a very simple viewing device such as a hand-held lens. Obviously it would be tedious and even injurious to read much continuous text in this way, but the method is well suited to the production of reference works, where dramatic savings in bulk and cost can be made without invoking the special techniques—for librarian and reader—associated with microcopy.

Filming and reading equipment: information retrieval
Libraries first entering the field of microcopy will doubtless content themselves initially with providing enough reading machines. Should they need to make microcopies of material in their possession, or to duplicate microcopies, they can rely with safety on the services of the large and reputable companies specialising in this work. Possibly the next stage is to buy simple microfiche duplicating equipment so that copies can be made for library users or for library stock if the original is elsewhere. If the volume of microfilming grows however, it may become economic, and more convenient, for the library to undertake its own filming. A straightforward planetary camera, with elementary stripping equipment to make microfiche might be the first buy. Even at this stage, the purchase of processing units, especially for roll film, may not be justified. The commercial companies will process rapidly any satisfactorily exposed film sent to them. It may be mentioned in passing that some new film materials and new processing methods allow for immediate dry development, so eliminating all processing delay.

The ordinary microfilm camera most likely to be used in libraries is dignified by the name of *planetary*. In essence it is no more than a 35mm or 16mm still camera mounted on a vertical coloum so that it can move up and down to alter the reduction ratio. It takes 100ft of film at one loading and has controlled lighting and exposure to ensure standard quality. It can photograph single sheets or books: for the latter there may be some special arrangement in the base-board to keep the double spread flat wherever the book is opened. The cost of a planetary camera does not put its purchase out of court for many libraries: equipment may be obtained for five or six times the cost of a good amateur camera, or about the same price as a small car. Much more expensive is the *step and repeat* camera used to make microfiches. Here the camera automatically records images one by one in a horizontal row, and then, like a typewriter carriage, moves down a line to start the next row. It is fed either with rectangles of film or with 105mm wide film which is later cut up into separate fiches. This latter method involves some wastage of film in loading and unloading the camera which is serious if only intermittent

34

Fig 3b: Microfiche reader

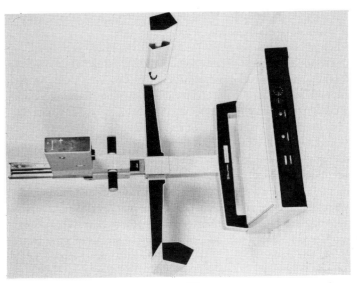

Fig 3a: Planetary microfilm camera

work is done. The cheapest type of microfilm camera—less than half the cost of the planetary—is the *flow* camera, but its use in libraries is restricted. It is a compact, table-top piece of equipment designed to take single sheet documents fed into a slot. The reduction ratio is fixed, but here duplex (two sided) filming is possible. It is cheap, speedy and convenient, and a library might well purchase if it had a special need for recording single sheet material.

Microform reading equipment varies widely in its purpose, specifications, and consequently price. Many machines can be bought for about the cost of a colour television set, but the very cheapest (ignoring hand-held magnifiers) are only a quarter of this expense. These are affectionately named 'cuddly' microfiche readers, so called because they are light and small enough to be held in the lap. As they are so cheap, they are ideal for issue to students from libraries. But here a warning is needed against too free acceptance of a manufacturer's description of his machine as 'portable'. Perhaps all that is meant is that it is not fixed to the floor and that it is just possible to stagger from one room to another with it. There are however small models which can be carried easily. But there are very few battery-operated readers and so freedom of use is restricted to the length of lead from an electric supply. Many machines are capable of taking both film and fiche, but the truly 'universal' machine (which will also take opaques) is dying. Indeed for reasons given under *Micro-opaque* above, it is difficult to obtain a low cost satisfactory reader for opaques.

A reader/printer goes one stage further than the microform reader as it also produces at the press of a button a full sized paper copy of the frame on the screen. A variety of photocopy methods are used for the print-out, and one technique (electrolytic) which is not found in photocopy. Reader/printers are of course much more expensive than simple reading equipment. Another range of machines—often extremely expensive—may be termed 'production printers' or 'enlarger printers'. These do not give an image on a screen but are usually intended for high volume production of full size copies from microforms. Thus one of these machines would automatically print out any required number of all or any selected frames of a microfiche. Another, of the highest possible importance to libraries, is the Xerox Copyflo system. This prints out microfilm to readable size, so a single copy of an out of print microfilmed book, for example, can be produced quickly and cheaply. The Copyflo apparatus is of such expense that only the largest national libraries would consider buying it, and in fact the manufacture of the equipment has been discontinued. It can still be used however on a service basis through such companies as University Microfilms. Most libraries are likely to restrict their purchases in this area to a few reader/printers, but even so, a word of warning is perhaps needed. It is natural for library users to prefer hard copy to microforms: the provision of print-out facilities may unleash an unwarranted demand for full size copies of almost everything. (Paper copies can be read at home so much more easily). But to accede to the demand would take away much of the economy which microtechniques bring.

The more expensive film readers have a motorised rapid winding system to save time in finding the required place on the film. Sometimes too, finding devices are incorporated so that it is unnecessary constantly to stop the film to find one's whereabouts. Apart from a simple footage meter these methods require some special preparation at the filming stage and may consist merely of blank frames regularly spaced so that the flashes which occur as the film is wound rapidly on the reader may be counted. Or horizontal lines between frames can move progressively upward as the film progresses: the height of the line against a scale on the reader indicating how far the film has wound through. Frames can also be counted optically and automatically by means of small opaque squares or 'blips' beneath the frames, but here a keyboard attachment is needed to key in the frame number required. Rapid retrieval devices do not apply only to film: the Micrographic Technology Corporation, for example, has recently introduced a system based on numbers of cartridges, each containing thirty microfiches. By the pressing of buttons the required frame is projected on the screen in three seconds.

These methods are no more than finding devices: they pre-suppose that the user knows which frame he wants. By contrast, information retrieval systems have the facility to search a store of information and select what is needed according to a range of enquiries which may be made of it. The complex analysis involved requires some form of subject coding or even a computer. A full scale treatment of mechanical information retrieval is outside the scope of this book; suffice it merely to refer to some categories of information retrieval systems which employ microforms as the storage medium for the information. Computer control—and therefore the facility for searching by subject or any other factor—can be applied to the optical 'blip' finding device referred to in the last paragraph. Other systems, for example the CARD equipment which stores 750 microfiches can similarly be operated simply by keyboarding the frame required or be linked to a computer. Fully computerised installations are extrémely expensive and have been used only experimentally or in large national libraries and agencies. An example is IBM's 'Walnut' using tiny microfiche 'chips' of 1mm in length. Other systems do not employ computers but some other means of coding the subject of a microfim frame or other unit of information. The simplest example—aperture cards—has already been referred to. Frequently a binary code in a chequer-board pattern denoting the subject is filmed side by side with the microcopy of the document to which it refers, and the retrieval machine is programmed to search for a certain pattern. The Rapid Selector—one of the first in the field—uses reels of microfilm 6000 feet long while Kodak Miracode has the usual 100 foot lengths and allows for a limited range of searching via a binary code on the film and a keyboard unit. Systems using microfiche rather than film include Filmorex and Kodak Minicard. Both use small fiche containing code and text.

COM (Computer output on microfilm)

A simplified account of COM, avoiding the technical complexities, is given here because of its importance in library cataloguing.

Computers deliver the information required from them either by ephemeral picture or text on a screen (a visual display unit) or in permanent form usually by an 'impact printer' which may be equated to a crude form of typewriter, automatically operated. COM is an alternative to the impact printer. The workings of a COM recorder are highly sophisticated, but one may think of the machine photographing the picture on the computer's visual display unit on to microfilm, so that the computer's permanent output is microfilm, not typed paper. There are other systems of recording but the output is the same. There is no need to go further into the mechanics of COM recorders as their cost is such that a library would not buy one but would rely on the services of a COM bureau. The cost of COM recorders is, however, reducing.

Of very much more importance is an understanding of the great benefits which COM brings. Indeed the only disadvantage, important to many, but possibly not to readers of this book, is that the output is not in an immediately readable form. This is no more than the general drawback of all microtexts, but given the right applications the advantages of COM are overwhelming.

Impact printers consume vast quantities of paper. The micro alternative not only saves dramatically on storage space, but conserves the use of paper which is becoming a scarce commodity rising steeply in price. Moreover there is often a need for the computer to produce more than one copy of its output simultaneously. Multiple part stationery for impact printers is expensive and there is a limit to the number of copies which can be produced at once. Copies are also indifferent in quality. But duplication of microcopy is so cheap that it is possible for a library to have a copy of its COM produced catalogue for each of its service points. The cheapness of the whole procedure is in fact such that frequent updating is feasible: a new COM film merely replaces the old, having had new material inserted by the computer, not by tedious manual filing. COM, too, scores in aesthetics. Admittedly it is not difficult to improve on the crude typography of the impact printer, but COM recorders, except the simplest, can manage both upper and lower case letters, and the most advanced handle graphics (line illustrations, graphs, plans etc). The final advantage is of less concern to the librarian using a COM service bureau, but COM has been claimed to be up to 30 times faster than an impact printer in operation. There is obviously an effect on throughput and therefore the cost to the customer.

A COM bureau will supply computer produced 16mm film ready inserted into cartridges or cassettes. Although the emphasis throughout this section has been on film, COM output can be on fiche; there are special forms with up to 48X reduction.

Design of originals for microforms
Most microfilming is done from material originally produced as hard copy: books, periodicals and all kinds of printed and typed matter. Clearly nothing can be done to alter the typography or page layout in such cases: this section is mainly concerned with those situations where an image is created specifically for microfilming, and economics are making these instances more frequent. But it may be said in passing that poor ready made originals can only produce poor microcopy. An example from the author's experience is of 5ins x 3ins micro-opaques being made from badly inked stencil duplicated originals. Filming with its reduction and enlargement on a reader must cause some degradation of the image. In the example cited the addition of an unsatisfactory opaque reader completed the recipe for user rejection of microforms.

It follows therefore that if the creation of the image is under the control of those responsible for microfilming, there is no excuse for unfilmable texts. Chapter VII deals with image creation for reprography in general, and applies perhaps even more to microcopy that the other forms. Certainly clarity and sharpness of text assume a crucial importance because of the reduction and enlargement involved, and generous and intelligent spacing of texts, especially headings, is one way in which typescript can make up for the lack of typographic variation found in printer's type.

One can afford, too, to make a generous allowance of space in the layout of a film or fiche for various devices to make reference to the information easier. For this purpose some slight increase in the space needed should not be denied in view of the great savings which microtexts confer in any event. Movement from frame to frame of a fiche or film is not as easy as turning to another page of a book and some conventions of book design should therefore be discarded. Notes and references accumulated at the end of a chapter will require annoying movement to a distant frame: they should instead be on the frame in which the reference is made. For the same reason *op cit* and *ibid* should be avoided unless the full information is on the same frame. Notes, diagrams and graphs useful at more than one place should be repeated where necessary. The same principle applies to contents pages and indexes, which certainly need not be confined to one per work, as in books. There is no need in most cases to go as far as the Omindex system which has an index to the whole work around the borders of each frame, but at least the fiche of a multi-fiche work should have information on the contents of the other fiches. And of course references to fiche frames should not give page numbers but the coordinates, *eg* B4 (Row B column 4). The frames themselves should be so lettered in any event to facilitate finding a frame relative to any other.

We have already discussed ciné and comic mode (see under *Reel microfilm* above, p27) and expressed a preference for the former. It opens up the possibilities of dispensing with page divisions, although some cameras are geared to make a break between frames. Fiche, too, can be arranged in a number of continuous vertical columns. Also previously mentioned is the need to keep all material one way up—it matters little in the printed book that an illustration runs up the length of a page and is at right angles to the text, but is much more disadvantageous in microform. It is this difference between the design needs of hard copy and those of microtexts which needs to be kept in mind.

CHAPTER IV

MICROCOPY—USES

This chapter attempts a rapid review of the uses to which microtexts are put in libraries and draws attention to the barriers to fuller exploitation with some indication of how these may be overcome. At some points there will be slight overlapping with material in Chapter III (*Microcopy—methods*). This is necessary not only for the sake of clarity, but because some readers, particularly students, may read this book selectively, and may wish to avoid the more technical flavour of the last chapter.

In 1944 Fremont Rider's *The scholar and the future of the research library* appeared. His vision of libraries consisting largely of micro-materials has not yet been achieved. It will be demonstrated later that the 'hard copy' book still has its place and that microforms bring problems as well as solve them: nevertheless many of the undoubted benefits of micromethods cannot yet be exploited to the full because of a lingering reluctance to accept texts in microform. Unfamiliarity and aversion on the part of library users inhibit greater production and employment of micromaterials and associated hardware. That very unfamiliarity would be overcome by greater use, and it is probable that economic and other factors will force libraries to embrace microtechniques more whole-heartedly. In turn the larger market will bring down the cost of machines which are at present rather highly priced in relation to their often simple mechanics. So, in short, we look for a breaking of the vicious circle. At the end of this chapter are some hopeful signs that we are perhaps nearing the point of breakthrough.

Saving space
Perhaps the most obvious use of microtexts in libraries is the saving of space by storing less used items in microform. Here only a small fraction of the full potential has as yet been realised. With a saving in storage space of some 95 per cent problems of the ever increasing growth of libraries could be solved for many years to come. Fremont Rider's

oft-quoted statistic of libraries doubling in size every 16 years would cease to be true. It must be remembered, however, that he was writing only of research libraries which do not discard significant amounts of material. But for any library the financial implications can be immense. Not only can building costs be avoided or delayed but with them the attendant expense of shelving and other equipment and overheads such as heating, lighting, cleaning and extra staffing. But this reason alone, powerful as it is, rarely forces libraries into the use of microforms: they still retain as much hard copy as they can.

Two aspects of space saving may be worth a special mention. Firstly there is an extra convenience and compactness caused by the standard format of micro materials: a series of different sized books, pamphlets or documents will waste space because shelves must be positioned to accommodate the largest volume. Secondly the miniaturisation of a library improves the reader's access to the information. For example the information required may well be in a fiche in a cabinet a few steps from the enquiry point: the full sized equivalent of a little used item is likely to be in a distant reserve store not immediately available. Such repositories could be in a basement store in the main library building—awkward enough when heavy volumes have to be fetched—but also likely to be in a separate building removed from the high costs of the city centre, as in the case of the University of London. Immediate access to information is therefore hampered.

For many years microfilming has been employed as a substitute for storing back numbers of periodicals, bound or unbound. Indeed librarians are sometimes persuaded to eliminate the cost of binding by discarding their paper copies in favour of microfilm at the time at which they would otherwise be bound. In many instances therefore the alternatives of a microfilm and paper version of a periodical exist side by side, and it is an interesting comment on the copyright implications of microcopy that there is frequently some arrangement whereby the micro version is available only to the subscriber to the paper edition. There is no doubt that microcopies, like photocopies, militate against the sale of originals, and despite the strictures of copyright acts and regulations much illicit micro-duplication of material in copyright is carried on. (See Chapter I p14).

Aids to library services: information retrieval
The economics of microtechniques are sufficiently flexible to comprehend full publishing ventures of multiple copies at one end of the scale, and the production of a single copy by a library for its own use at the

other. In the latter context libraries may guard against loss of, or damage to, valuable originals by making a microcopy. Use of copies by other libraries could follow, but this is not the primary aim. Examples are the American Council of Learned Societies' wartime Rockefeller project of microfilming British material at risk of destruction from bombing, and the microfilming of local newspapers to save the wear and tear on the rapidly deteriorating paper of the original. Manchester Public Libraries was a pioneer in its filming of the (Manchester) Guardian.

Before going on to micro publishing, one must mention the other uses libraries make of microfilm, often of single copies only, to help in their services. These range from the fairly recent developments of COM produced catalogues which will be dealt with later in this chapter, to the library housekeeping job of the recording of loans. A large number of public libraries now employ the photocharging system whereby a record of a loan is made on 16mm microfilm. The result has been an elimination of the once familiar queues at the 'in' counter at busy periods. But it must be admitted that no issue system is perfect: photocharging causes a little hold up at the outgoing desk, and difficulties concerning reservation of books and overdue reminders have necessitated different and not always satisfactory routines.

A valuable feature of library service is the facility to obtain material on loan from another library. This could be items otherwise unobtainable, or uneconomic for the home library to stock. Microforms confer great advantages in this service. The lending library, by sending a copy, does not deprive its own readers of the use of a volume; furthermore it drastically reduces postage costs and avoids all risk of damage to, or loss of the original. Indeed the costs of microtechniques are so modest that frequently a microfiche is sent for retention, giving the further bonus of cutting out the administrative cost of recording and recalling a loan. The British Library Lending Division, (formerly the National Lending Library for Science and Technology) operates this system. It might be mentioned again that the full success of this method depends on the complete acceptance of microforms by the user libraries, implying a sufficiency of viewing equipment. Giving away a microcopy can also be used instead of loans *within* a library: an example of this is given at the end of this chapter.

The density of information storage on microfilm makes it a natural adjunct to mechanical systems of information retrieval. There have been many such devices, from the early Rapid Selector through IBM's 'Walnut', Minicard and Filmorex, to the more contemporary CARD equipment of

Image Systems. But one cannot say that mechanical information retrieval is widespread in libraries. Equipment is naturally enough expensive and economies of scale seem unlikely. Use is largely confined to large specialised libraries and information centres, an interesting example being the use of Walnut by the USA Central Intelligence Agency (CIA). It is, however, surprising that the simpler, widely available equipment has not been better exploited for library use. For example an aperture card could easily be punched with a classification number relating to a document or abstract on the 35mm inserted frame. Perhaps this will yet come now that 8-up aperture cards are here; the growing standardisation of their use for patents is encouraging.

Acquisition of materials: micropublishing
Libraries acquire material in many forms; books, pamphlets, periodicals, illustrations, tapes, slides etc. The librarian who ignores microtexts is indeed foolish as there is now a great wealth of material in this form, much of it otherwise quite unobtainable, or obtainable only with great difficulty and at a high price. Acquisition of micro materials by a library can at one end of the scale result from a request for a single microcopy to another library which contains a rare or unique item—perhaps a manuscript or an early printed book. At the other end of the scale we are in the realms of micropublishing, where established firms offer a range of microtexts for sale as a commercial venture. By use of Xerox Copyflo a microfilm can be converted into a readable sized book at remarkably low cost. Although Copyflo equipment is no longer in production it is still in use. Its enormous bibliographical importance in being able to produce 'reprints in an edition of one' will doubtless ensure a replacement and so a continuance of this facility. (See Chapter V p68.)

A wide spectrum of physical forms of microtext are on offer in the micropublishing field, particularly various forms of opaque and fiche, the latter developing, the former dying. One might usefully distinguish between the types intended for high volume production and those employed when only few copies are required. Opaques, particularly the offet-litho Readex Microprint, are economic only when an edition of some size is called for. While transparencies are generally cheaper for small runs, we now have the sophisticated high-reduction ultrafiches which again must have a sale of some hundreds to be viable. These high volume formats may contain long runs of periodicals, government documents, or 'package libraries' such as issued by the (American) Encyclopedia Brittanica. These

44

last are more popular in the USA than in Britain where possibly the originals are more accessible and where librarians may more resent the 'package' nature of the transaction taking selection out of their hands. Also it is understood that American colleges often have the need to demonstrate the richness of their library collections in order to be accredited to run certain courses. The relatively cheap micro package library is a convenient and economical way to satisfy this requirement. An interesting British 'package' is available from Harvester Primary Social Sources of Brighton, namely the entire output of several hundred British pressure groups on microfiche and indexed. The same company is now publishing on fiche the archives of the Labour Party and the TUC (Trades Union Congress). These are good examples of the value of micropublishing in supplying material otherwise unobtainable, indeed from unpublished sources. Even when hard copy is available as an alternative—from the new or secondhand markets—micro versions are dramatically less expensive; perhaps only a fifth of the price of the originals.

Low volume micropublishing, on film and particularly standard microfiche, demonstrates its viability at very low numbers of copies by even merging into 'potential publishing'. For example a publishing organisation may not make a fiche of a university thesis until an order comes in.

Before leaving micropublishing reference must be made to an important and fairly new development known as micro-litho or miniaturised print. Here a low reduction lithographic print is made on paper and can be read with the naked eye or a simple hand-held magnifier. An excellent example is the full 13 volume Oxford English Dictionary reduced to 2 volumes at a 2X reduction, and selling at one third of the price of the original. The example is typical in that it is a work of reference. While readers would find this kind of reduced size print trying when reading long passages of continuous text, the small type size is acceptable when consulting brief entries in a dictionary. Indeed the work is easier to use in two rather than thirteen volumes as users of a dictionary often have to refer from one entry to another. One can go further and say that the difficulty of finding the exact place and moving back and forth within the conventional fiche or film is an inherent drawback of micro-texts which miniaturised print does not share. In another way, too, micro-litho is an exception to the general rule of microtechniques, and this confers a most weighty advantage. No viewing apparatus is required (or only the simplest of hand lenses) and it will be seen later that the necessity for such hardware is a major factor in the slowness of the acceptance of microforms in libraries. With these advantages micro-litho could develop fast, particularly at a time when book production costs, (the price of paper being a significant item) are rising steeply.

COM catalogues

We may now turn to an especially encouraging feature of the use of micro-methods in libraries—the recent interest in library catalogues in microform. This development started with the introduction of computer-produced catalogues during the 1960's, for example at several public libraries in London. Perhaps a major reason for this change was the creation of the new London boroughs, bringing together libraries with existing catalogues in incompatible formats. These catalogues were printed out on to paper by the computer's impact printer unit. Nowadays the catalogue is computer generated but is produced in the form of cassetted 16mm microfilm. All the advantages of COM over impact printers are gained—immense saving of paper bulk and cost, easy and cheap duplication for each service point, and frequent updating is feasible. Of course a conventional manually produced card catalogue can be filmed to save space and to provide duplicates easily. This can be on 16mm cassettes and compatible with a COM produced catalogue, as at Birmingham University library. The use of cassettes as the most common format is worth a mention. Open reel microfilm with its need for threading up on a viewer would render the system impracticable for use by the public. The choice therefore was between cassetted film and fiche. The latter has some adherents but it is easy to lose or mis-file a fiche. There is mixed reaction by library users to consulting a catalogue in microform, but any opposition should be weighed against not only the great advantages of the system, but the general reluctance of the public to use any catalogue, whatever its format. It must be admitted, however, that whereas browsing in a catalogue may be possible in book form, it is virtually impossible in the micro equivalent.

The other notable COM catalogue development is the *Books in English* service provided by the British National Bibliography (British Library, Bibliographical Services Division). Here, in conjunction with the Library of Congress, British and American new publications are, via the MARC service tapes, outputted on to PCMI fiches, providing an exceedingly compact and comprehensive bibliographical conspectus. The author remembers being asked some years ago by a representative of NCR what would be the library reaction to a fiche with a 150:1 reduction ratio. Regrettably I replied that as conventional microforms could save 95% of space I could see no use for anything which went further. While this may be true enough for much library material, PCMI scores when very large amounts of data are needed on one or two fiches for ease of handling, reference and replacement. This medium is therefore ideal for a world-wide bibliographical service such as *Books in English* with its need for very large storage capacity and facilities for frequent updating. Non-library applications of PCMI—such as catalogues of motor parts—find the same needs met.

Disadvantages of microtexts
Some enthusiasts for micro methods pay insufficient attention to the draw-backs of their use in libraries, while many librarians use the disadvantages as excuses for refusal to exploit them. One handicap may be briefly stated—the lack of sufficient standardisation. The incompatibility of cassettes is an example. This could be eliminated, but another disadvantage of the use of microtexts is inherent. This is the inability to allow for browsing, a much more significant fault than may be realised. The approach to information through browsing (or serendipity as it is unnecessarily known in professional writings) is of much wider value than merely finding interesting leisure reading by chance gazing at public library shelves. It has repeatedly been shown that new scientific discoveries have resulted from the cross-fertilisa-tion of one discipline with another, perhaps by the importation of an idea or a technique from chance reading outside the specific subject.

The major drawback of microtexts, however, —also inherent—is the necessity of using a viewing device—a piece of hardware which must always accompany text and user. Compared with the instant readability of the conventional book, microforms are only indirectly readable: to many li-brary users the tiresome and inconvenient requirement to find and use a perhaps unfamiliar piece of gadgetry is enough to disuade them from using microtexts as they should. Hard copy can be read in the train, in bus queues, at odd moments between other jobs, and in bed. There is evidence from studies made of the reading habits of scientific research workers that the majority of professional reading is done outside working hours and away from the office or library. Microtexts can never match the ease and flexibility of use of conventional print, but the development of really cheap, really portable viewing apparatus can go a long way to multiply the situations in which microforms can be an acceptable alternative. Simple 'cuddly' microfiche readers (so called because they can be rested on the knees when seated) may be obtained for half the cost of the least expen-sive table models. While this seems cheap, it must be remembered that an uncomplicated slide projector for amateur home use sells for far less yet

47

its optics are very similar.   The difference in price is presumably due to the presence or lack of volume production to achieve economy. Demand and price are therefore related: a very cheap portable would enable libraries to loan machines freely for use outside the library, and the numbers required would have a favourable effect on prices. A further boost to the use of portables would come from the development of satisfactory and lightweight battery models, for otherwise, however portable the machine, its use is limited to the radius of a lead from a power socket.

It may be thought that reader/printers provide an answer to the problem of reading texts where no viewing equipment is available or possible. They do provide this answer, but at some cost. The machines are much more expensive than simple readers, and the running costs of sensitive paper etc must be added. To use reader/printers widely would therefore take away some of the economy which microtechniques offer. Moreover, unless strictly controlled, library users would call for hard copy print-out at all times, whether really needed for reading at home or not. Not only would costs escalate but the much desired acclimatisation of library users to microforms would never happen.

The librarian committed to exploiting micro materials must not only consider investing in a multitude of portable readers for loan, but must ensure that his library is fully equipped with an adequate number of viewers for use on the premises. By 'adequate' is meant sufficient for peak rather than normal demand if library users are not to be frustrated at the busiest times. It is annoying if the library does not have immediately available the material which is required: doubly so if it is available but unusable because of the non-availability of the machine to read it. Furthermore, some users may even have a need to use more than one microform reader at once. We have already mentioned that finding the required place on a film or fiche may be tedious, and to avoid repeatedly changing over fiches or films, the user who needs to refer to more than one text at once may wish to have them separately set up on different readers.

User resistance may largely be unreasonable prejudice—reading microtexts does not, for example, cause the eyestrain it once did when quality of originals, filming and design of viewers were poor. But user resistance is still a fact. To quote one librarian speaking of the situation in his university library a few years ago: 'We use microforms purely and simply . . . as substitutes for the real thing . . . I prefer hard copy'. Also ' . . . if one is going to save 50 per cent on cost one may lose 50 per cent of readers (users)'. (Linton, W D 'The economics of microfilm in libraries and information centres' *in* Plumb, P W *ed The economics of microfilming and document reproduction* Microfilm Association of Great Britain, 1969.) The vicious circle must be broken. If libraries were more adventurous in providing micro material user resistance would gradually be overcome. More publications would appear in microtext only making it necessary for librarians to buy in this format. In turn library users would have to use microtexts or forgo the information they contain.

Hope for the future
There are now signs that the use of microtexts in libraries is becoming more widespread. Some of the recent developments mentioned in this chapter are indications, and the various organisations listed in Chapter VIII are having an effect in spreading the word and giving information. Some libraries, too, are now fully committed to making the maximum use of microtechniques. An example personally known to the author is Hatfield Polytechnic; not surprising in view of the fact that its previous librarian was G H Wright, a pioneer in many respects, who also founded the National Reprographic Centre for documentation at Hatfield. Another example is the library of the (British) Consumers' Association, publishers of *Which?* Here files of press cuttings and working files of documents used during investigations are being converted to jacketed fiche. (This format is selected for its ease of updating). Not only will much space be saved, but access to information will be transformed. Instead of the loan of files to investigators with its attendant need for an issue system, and the risk of unavailability if the material is already on loan, a duplicate fiche is made for every request. Thus the researcher has the information for as long as he wishes: indeed, if desired he can build up his own permanent library! For its success the system depends on having a fiche reader on every researcher's desk.

The above example demonstrates several of the points made in this chapter—the need for abundant viewing equipment for instance. It also illustrates a special situation in which user resistance can be overcome. In the 'open' readership of the public or academic library readers have a choice of using microtexts or not. In the more 'closed' community of a specialised library it is easier to impose micromethods on the users if the decision is made to do so. But in all kinds of library inevitable pressures will foster the greater use of microtechniques, particularly where a clear and not too long-term financial advantage can be seen (as in COM catalogues) or where essential material is otherwise quite unobtainable.

But the greatest hope for the future lies, as always, with the younger generation. While upbringing on the traditional book has made older readers wary of new techniques, the young people now at school or university are more familiar with technology and less wedded to the book as an exclusive source of information. They watch television at home, their leisure activities may involve the use of tape recorders and ciné cameras, and doubtless in their formal education they will have been taught through the medium of various audio-visual methods. Microtexts will not seem so strange to them.

While the use of microforms in libraries will undoubtedly increase, it will be obvious from what has been stated in this chapter that it would be naïve to forecast the demise of the traditional book. The disadvantages of microtexts, indicated above, show why. A parallel may be found in transport, which like recorded information is an increasing activity. Micro methods like air travel are increasing their business in a totally expanding market, but there will always be a place for the more traditional methods where the newer techniques are less appropriate. Books, like ships, have their own advantages of usefulness and, indeed, beauty.

CHAPTER V

PHOTOCOPY

While microtechniques are virtually straight photography, photocopy is an adaptation of photography to achieve speed and cheapness.

It is of course technically feasible merely to photograph documents with a camera and to use the resulting prints as one would photocopies, but a look at the procedures involved will quickly demonstrate the extreme slowness and the expense. While any type of camera could be used it should be of good quality and will therefore be expensive. In roll-film cameras all the exposures on the film must be complete before any development can be done—most frustrating if a single quick copy is wanted. When the film is unloaded from the camera it must be developed, rinsed, fixed, washed and dried. We are then only at the negative stage. Negatives must be exposed on to photographic paper to make prints, and the prints developed, rinsed, fixed, washed and dried as before. All this processing could take hours, building up a huge labour cost.

Photocopy gains in speed over photography in several ways. Naturally one can copy a single document without waiting for a film to be expended. But the most important speed up is in the truncating of processing time. There is no development at all in some processes: in others it is reduced to one pass through a machine. Wet chemical baths are a nuisance and the drying time slows up the availability of the copy, so after some experience of 'semi-dry' processing (or 'semi-wet' if one is a pessimist) we now find that most modern processes have completely dry development. Sometimes the penalty of speedy development is lack of permanence in the copies. Even with the fastest processing, or no processing at all, some methods have the disadvantage shared by photography that they are two stage methods, that is, the exposure of the original results in an unusable intermediary (for example a negative) which must be re-copied to produce the final copy. There is obviously an advantage of speed and economy in one-stage methods.

51

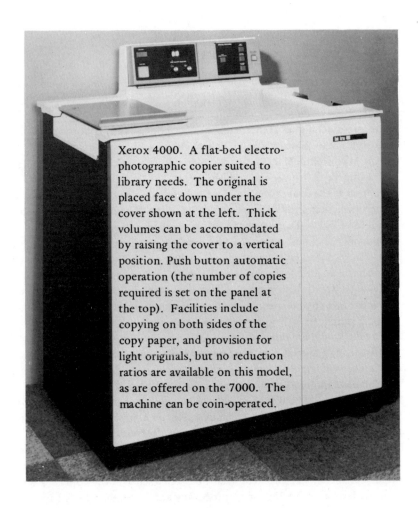

Xerox 4000. A flat-bed electro-photographic copier suited to library needs. The original is placed face down under the cover shown at the left. Thick volumes can be accommodated by raising the cover to a vertical position. Push button automatic operation (the number of copies required is set on the panel at the top). Facilities include copying on both sides of the copy paper, and provision for light originals, but no reduction ratios are available on this model, as are offered on the 7000. The machine can be coin-operated.

Fig 4: Flat-bed photocopier

Economy is achieved in photocopy by two main approaches, apart from the economy in labour costs which comes from increased speed. One is the substitution of paper for the more expensive film used in photography. This means that even in a two stage process, the negative intermediary is on paper, unlike photography. The other economy is by dispensing with the camera in many processes. These 'contact' methods use a simple light box for exposure and as there is no lens involved, only copies of the same size as the original are possible. There is then, a price to pay for the economy which photocopy achieves over photography: it is less versatile in that it can copy only flat documents; it is often restricted to same-size copying; and its rendering of tone illustrations usually suffers badly compared with photography.

This chapter assumes that copies will be made in black and white, (or occasionally some colour other than black) but not in full natural

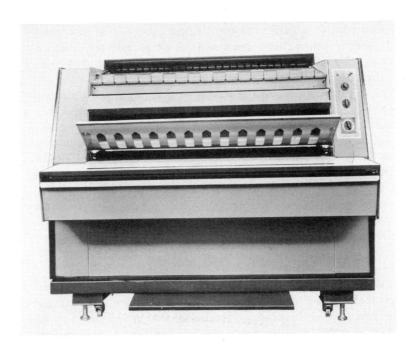

Fig 5: Rotary photocopier (Dyeline). In rotary copiers such as this, the originals, in sheet form, are fed into the machine through a slot.

colours. Colour photocopiers have long been heralded, but they have now arrived in the USA and are about to be introduced into Britain. Naturally copies in colour are very expensive, but they could be of great benefit to some applications, such as design, fashion and advertising work. Libraries and other users may find their need for coloured copies infrequent, so that it would be out of the question to install such an expensive system. They would be likely to satisfy their intermittent needs by recourse to putting work out to the manufacturer on a service basis, or use of an 'instant print' shop. Such shops may well be the major customers for the machines, at least until the cost comes down.

Before looking at individual methods of photocopy a few comments are needed on the major processes they employ, by which they are conventionally grouped. A simple chart appears on p55: certainly other relationships can be found, and diagrams found elsewhere are often more complicated. Suffice it to say here that there are four groups of methods which are divided by the chemistry of the process, often the nature of the sensitive surface on which the copy is made. There are a) photographic, the sensitive coating being silver halide as in conventional photography, b) diazo or dyeline c) thermographic or heat copying and d) electrostatic, or as it is now termed electrophotographic copying, which is near to sweeping the board, at least as far as library copying is concerned. The other processes (a—c) are however worth a brief mention as they still have some specialist uses. Photocopying may also be divided by use or non use of a lens system, referred to in the last paragraph. Most methods are 'contact' or non-camera; the exceptions are Photostat and also electrophotographic which usually employs a lens or mirror system although only some machines give variable size copies. Projection printing (ie enlargement) is possible in some of the other processes, eg photo stabilisation, but for simplicity this is ignored in the chart as the typical library photocopy application is by contact.

Photostat

The most appropriate starting place for a description of photocopy methods is a brief comment on Photostat. This is not because of the present day importance of the process, for although it is still used, the equipment is no longer in production. Its significance lies in demonstrating the earliest adaptation of photography for photocopy purposes. As with other developments which are first in their field the name 'Photostat' is widely misused as a synonym for a photocopy of any sort. In fact it is a Kodak trade name for this particular process. In a sentence,

Fig 6: Simplified chart showing relationship of photocopy processes
(Alternative names are given in brackets)

	CAMERA PROCESSES (Variable sized copies)	NON-CAMERA OR CONTACT PROCESSES (Same sized copies)
PHOTOGRAPHIC PROCESSES (Silver halide)	Photostat	Negative/positive ("reflex") Chemical (diffusion) transfer Autopositive (direct positive)
NON-PHOTOGRAPHIC PROCESSES		Dyeline (diazo)
		Thermographic (heat) copying − "Thermofax" − heat transfer − dual spectrum
	Electro photographic copying may give fixed or reduced sized copies.	

Photostat is no more than a large camera which photographs on to paper
instead of film. This is the modification for cheapness, but in other respects it is pure photography with its advantages and disadvantages—an
expensive camera: processing with wet chemicals: high quality: the ability
to vary the size of the prints. Also it produces a negative at the first stage;
recopying is needed to make a positive. Negative copies are however usable
in this process for the following reason. Any camera produces an image reversed from left to right, and therefore unreadable. This is of no significance
on film as the image can be read by turning over the negative. As this is not
possible with a paper negative a prism is incorporated in the Photostat sys
tem which turns the image round to make it readable. These right-reading
negative prints are perfectly acceptable, except where tone illustrations
are included. Photostat may still be of value where high quality large
sized prints are required, for example of newspaper pages.

55

Fundamentals of contact copying

With the exception of electrophotographic copying which is treated separately, all other photocopy processes are non-camera or contact. As explained in Chapter I (p13) two types of contact apparatus are usually available for each process. These are *rotary* which will take only single sheets, not books, and *flat-bed* or *book copiers*. As the latter will take all kinds of material they are the natural choice for libraries. Whatever the type of copier however and whatever the process three different techniques of exposure are possible. The choice of these techniques is determined by the kind of material to be copied. In turn the technique used determines whether or not the process is to be one-stage or two-stage and therefore has a crucial influence on expense. The three exposure techniques are as follows:

Direct exposure is the simplest. As will be seen from Fig 7a, light shines through the background areas of the original but is prevented from penetrating by the text areas. The background areas of the copy paper are therefore affected by light. In photographic copying methods they would turn black after development, giving a negative: in other processes

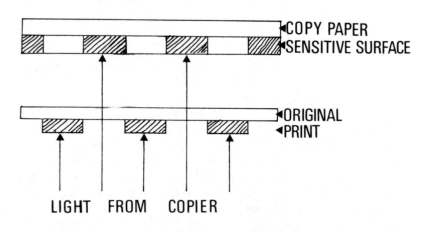

Produces 'right reading' POS or NEG according to paper used. Conditions: original must be translucent 'single sided'—ie not books

Fig 7a: Direct exposure

such as dyeline a positive copy would result. Whether positive or negative, the image would be readable, *ie* the right way round. One can think of direct exposure as merely 'casting a shadow' of the original on to the copy paper. This therefore gives a one stage process, which, as we have seen, is highly desirable on grounds of speed and economy. But this technique suffers from grave disadvantages which make it unusable for much photocopy work. It will be seen that the light must pass through the original: obviously therefore the paper must be thin and translucent enough for this to be possible, also print must be only one side of the paper, (otherwise a jumble of both sides would be recorded on the copy!) Many library materials like books do not, of course, conform to this requirement of 'translucent one-sided originals'.

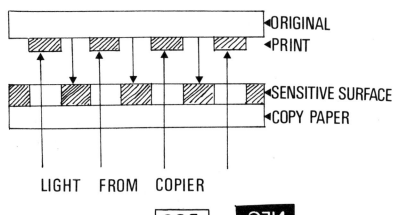

Produces 'wrong reading' 209 or NEG according to paper used. Needs a second stage to convert to right reading but takes double sided and opaque materials—ie books

Fig 7b: Reflex exposure

To overcome this problem *reflex exposure* is used. The reflex technique can copy anything because, as will be seen from Fig 7b, the light from the copier does not pass through the original but is reflected from the surface of it. As in direct exposure, whether a positive or negative copy is produced will depend on the chemistry of the process used. But reflex has its own disadvantage. Note that the original and the copy paper are face to face: inevitably a reversed, unreadable or mirror image will result, in the same way that printer's type is reversed so that it will print the right way round when brought face to face with paper. Therefore reflex exposure means two stage copying, as the first copy produced must be re-copied to obtain a right reading final copy.

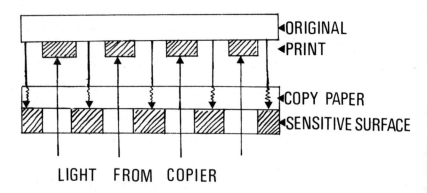

Takes opaque and double sided originals and gives a right reading copy in one step but, as the image has to travel through the thickness of the paper, copy is fuzzy and the copy paper must be thin

Fig 7c: Reversed reflex exposure

Reversed reflex exposure (the term is not in general use) provides a means of overcoming the two-stage disadvantage of reflex but only with considerable loss in quality. In this technique the copy paper is turned to face the same way as the original, *ie* towards the light source. As before, the image is formed by reflecting light from the surface of the original, but in reversed reflex the image must penetrate the thickness of the paper backing on the copy paper before it reaches the sensitive surface. For this reason copy papers using this exposure technique are very thin, sometimes unsatisfactorily unsubstantial, to minimise the diffraction by the paper fibres which makes the image unsharp. Even so, some spread of the image always occurs, so copies made by this technique are not of the best quality.

58

In both reflex and reversed reflex exposure it may be wondered why the light from the copier does not fog or spoil the copy paper, as it is flooded with light, only some of which passes through and is reflected back by the original. The answer is that the threshold of light sensitivity of the copy paper can be so formulated that only the double amount of light (direct from the copier and reflected back from the original) is enough to record an image. Most copy papers can be so formulated, but dyeline papers cannot, so dyeline copying is confined to direct exposure. Also for this reason the operator's latitude in exposure error may be much reduced. In reversed reflex sometimes one can do no better than produce a copy which bears dark grey text on a light grey background!

Photographic methods
We can now apply the principles explained above to individual copying methods and firstly to that group of processes using photographic or silver halide paper. The earliest of these methods was little more than the substitution of a contact light source for the Photostat camera. Unfortunately this process is known as 'reflex' which confuses with the technique of exposure, pervasive through all contact methods, which was set out in the last section. For clarity, therefore, the name *Negative/positive* will be used. If exposure is by the direct method a readable negative results: if by reflex, which must be used for most originals, an unreadable negative which must be recopied. Originally the development was in trays of wet chemicals, but later semi-dry processing was introduced whereby the copy paper was fed speedily over rollers carrying highly concentrated chemicals. As the paper never became saturated it dried quickly. This adaptation is termed *photo-stabilisation*. Negative/positive gives good quality and is better for halftones than many other types of photocopy. The negative can of course be re-used for making further positive copies of the same original.

Transfer methods were introduced to speed up the production of the final positive copy where a reflex exposure has to be made. The necessary two stages become virtually one. The copy paper is exposed in contact with the original as before, but instead of developing it out at once to an unreadable negative, it is placed face to face with a special positive sheet of paper, (not itself sensitive to light) and the two are passed, sandwiched together, through the developer. The small amount of solution trapped between the papers develops the negative and chemicals migrate across to the facing sheet to form a positive image. After a few seconds the two are separated and the negative discarded. Thus the process is known informally as the 'peel-apart' method but more officially as *chemical transfer* or *diffusion transfer* to distinguish from mechanical or gelatin transfer (Verifax) which is now defunct. The process is prone to high wastage, but a strong black image is possible. At one time this was the most widely used of all photocopy methods. It is still in use for making lithographic plates, but for ordinary copying it is being eclipsed by the electrophotographic process. Note that the negative cannot be re-used: the whole process must be repeated if a second copy of the same original is needed. An earlier 'multicopy' system of re-usable negatives (they had to be used at once and could not be stored) does not survive.

The *autopositive* or *direct positive* process breaks the photographic rules. The result of exposure and development is a positive, not a negative image. If direct exposure is used the result is a readable positive, obviously much more desirable than the readable negative produced by the first of our photographic processes. But most originals demand reflex exposure, and in this case the result would be an unreadable positive, which has no advantage (except as a cheap dyeline transparency—see p63) over an unreadable negative; indeed it is less useful, as autopositive paper is more expensive than negative working material. It is because of this that 'reversed reflex' exposure is used, as explained on p58. This means that a readable positive is obtainable from all kinds of original in one stage, but as noted previously, good quality is difficult to obtain and the copy paper must be thin.

An interlude on costing
This book eschews detailed costing figures for reasons given in the preface and Chapter II. It is however useful at this point to use the three photographic methods just described to illustrate the effect on costs of one stage and two stage methods, and methods which re-use the intermediary for further copies. It must be stressed that the figures given bear no relationship to cents, pence or any monetary unit; they are employed to demonstrate the calculation without recourse to algebraic symbols. The assumption is made for simplicity that a piece of photocopy paper costs 4 units, whatever its kind. (This is not quite true as we have seen that autopositive is a little more expensive). Also assumed is that reflex exposure is employed in negative/positive, reversed reflex in autopositive.

It will be seen from the table that autopositive is the cheapest throughout. Using only one piece of paper for each copy the cost per copy remains steady however many copies are made. Chemical transfer, using

Fig 8: Comparative costing of photographic contact methods using reflex exposure (reversed reflex in the case of Autopositive). Units are arbitrary.

NO OF COPIES FROM ONE ORIGINAL	NEGATIVE/ POSITIVE		CHEMICAL TRANSFER		AUTOPOSITIVE	
	TOTAL COST	COST/ COPY	TOTAL COST	COST/ COPY	TOTAL COST	COST/ COPY
1	8	8.0	8	8.0	4	4.0
2	12	6.0	16	8.0	8	4.0
3	16	5.3	24	8.0	12	4.0
4	20	5.0	32	8.0	16	4.0
5	24	4.8	40	8.0	20	4.0
6	28	4.7	48	8.0	24	4.0
7	32	4.6	56	8.0	28	4.0
8	36	4.5	64	8.0	32	4.0
9	40	4.4	72	8.0	36	4.0
10	44	4.4	80	8.0	40	4.0

two pieces of paper per copy, is exactly twice as expensive. Indeed for multiple copies it is quite uneconomic compared with negative/positive (and incidentally, many other processes). In negative/positive two sheets of paper are expended for the first copy, but as the negative is re-usable, the second and subsequent copies each add only one sheet of paper to the cost. Thus the cost per copy reduces the more copies are made but the reduction levels out. However, after three or four copies there is not a great deal of difference in cost between negative/positive and autopositive. When we remember the slight extra expense of autopositive paper and the vastly better quality of negative/positive, the latter has the advantage.

Dyeline or diazo

There is a slight technical difference in the development process between dyeline and diazo, but for our purposes the terms are taken as interchangeable. As a non-photographic process, dyeline is positive working. It is also the cheapest of all photocopy methods, employing very inexpensive sensitive paper, (although the machines can be costly). These two factors would seem to make dyeline desirable, but unfortunately it has a large drawback for library applications. It operates only on direct exposure (see p56) so that its use is confined to reproducing single sided translucent originals. Its major application is for engineering drawings which of course satisfy these requirements. Indeed dyeline is a development of the blue-print process.

The sensitive side of diazo paper is covered with a yellow compound which is destroyed by light. The light must be ultra-violet, so that paper can be handled safely in normal room lighting. When exposed in the photocopier the ultra-violet light shining through the white paper of the original destroys the diazo except where the black text 'casts a shadow' and protects it. The result is a faint positive image in yellow on white paper. (It is the right way round because direct exposure has been used). As the faint image is barely visible a developing stage is needed to bring the image to a darker colour—typically blue, but other colours are available. The developing agent may with some papers be merely heat, but it is usually either a liquid applied by rollers, or ammonia vapour. If the last method is used the pungent fumes must be ducted away to the open air: this will add to the problems and expense of installation. As noted before, machines are rather expensive, because of the ultra-violet light requirement. The cheapest are about twice the cost of a transfer copier. Moreover no flat-bed (book copiers) are now available. There would, in fact, be no point, as dyeline is unable to copy from books because they need a reflex exposure.

It may seem that in a book for librarians, dyeline, because of its disadvantages, does not warrant a mention. But there are some library situations in which it could be appropriately used. As dyeline is so cheap, if say 20 copies are required of one original which calls for reflex exposure, it may be worth while to make a transparency of the original and reproduce cheap dyeline copies from it. A transparency can be made by one of several of the other photography processes. Chemical transfer gives a good dense image, and as it is usually produced on clear film rather than paper, only a small exposure is required in making the dyeline prints with a consequent saving in time. (Rotary photocopiers vary exposure by the speed at which papers pass around the cylindrical light source). The cheapest dyeline transparency (translucency rather) is a reversed (unreadable) positive copy made by the autopositive process (see p60). Being on paper it is cheap, and its mirror-reading nature means that it must be placed emulsion to emulsion with the dyeline paper. This ensures a sharper image than if a thickness of paper intervened between the two sensitive surfaces.

It is, however, doubtful if many libraries would bother to use dyeline via the intermediary of a transparency unless they had a demand for a consistent number of copies from one original which made dyeline particularly economic. Electrophotographic copying is likely to win—as it does so often—on the grounds of speed and convenience, but this may not be so if the organisation already had dyeline equipment installed to serve other needs. In the few cases where no intermediate transparency is required, dyeline is of course much more competitive. This could occur when the organisation controls the making of the original in the first place. Two examples may be given. The first is demonstrated by the words 'This paper is suitable for dyeline copying' printed at the foot of letters etc. sent out by the British government. Typists are instructed to use only one side of the paper so that should a copy be needed in the future, dyeline can be used. For best results a special typing paper such as Diazobond may be used. This is of normal appearance but transmits ultra-violet light readily so shortening dyeline exposure time. The second example comes from the author's experience in a special library of a steel-making company. A major task was the preparation of literature searches, often of many pages in length. The library stored several carbon copies of each in case of future repeat demand. But many were never wanted again, and the multiple carbons took up storage space. If there was a call for the same subject again, updating had to be carried out on a messy carbon. All this was replaced by a dyeline system whereby the literature search was originally typed on translucent paper, and any updatings would be done on this (cutting and insertion was possible). The library user requesting the literature search and any repeat requests were satisfied by dyeline copies.

Thermographic (heat) copying
There are three current methods within this group, all sharing the same fundamental principles. In contrast to dyeline which makes use of an ultra-violet light source, thermographic copying requires infra-red light, from the other end of the spectrum. When infra-red light strikes the metallic or carbon ink of the image on the original, heat is generated and reflected back on to the sensitive surface of the copy paper to form the

image. No development stage is required, Note that the change from infra-red light to heat will happen only if the ink of the original has a metallic or carbon content. In practice this means black ink as most coloured inks are vegetable dyes. The effect is that heat copying is 'colour blind', *ie*, colours on the original do not reproduce at all. This serious drawback, which would make nonsense of, say, a periodical article with coloured headings and diagrams, is overcome in the dual spectrum variant of thermographic copying, but only at the expense of making it a two stage process.

Thermographic copying was first introduced by the 3M company under the trade name *Thermofax*. At the time of its inception push-button electrophotographic copiers had not been developed: its main rival was transfer copying with its messy chemical processing. Since heat methods need no development, Thermofax scored heavily in speed, cleanliness and convenience. 'A copy in 4 seconds' was the boast, and the successful bid was to capture markets for the copying of office documents. Almost all equipment was well-styled rotary machines for desk top use: the one flat bed book copier produced did not provide good enough contact for satisfactory copies. On other counts, too, the original Thermofax process was not high in quality. To achieve a right reading result from a reflex exposure (see p58) the reversed reflex technique must be used and this inevitably means a somewhat fuzzy image and a very thin copy paper. Thermofax paper is brittle and difficult to file. Furthermore the bonus of lack of development has its own drawback. The copy paper remains sensitive to heat and will slowly blacken if left exposed to the sun. Also copies can be added to by subsequent copying on them: in some situations this can be an advantage as the manufacturers claim: in others there is the crucial disadvantage of lack of security, in that a seemingly authentic copy of a document may have bogus additions on it. In all, Thermofax has a mixture of merit and demerit. It was good for its time but now survives mainly as an excellent method for making transparencies for overhead projection (or dyeline). Because the copy is made on film, the unsharpness inherent in reversed reflex exposure is not in evidence. It can also prepare stencils for wax stencil duplicating.

An interesting variation on Thermofax—though little used because of the concurrent rise of electrophotographic copying—is the *heat-transfer* method. This is sometimes called the Eichner process from the company first introducing it. Here the copy paper itself is not sensitive to heat, but a sheet of dyed wax is placed next to the ordinary paper which will receive the copy. The heat generated by the infra-red light on the text melts the wax which adheres in the shape of the image to the copy paper. The two are then peeled apart. Naturally the process is colour-blind, and again the copy paper must be thin, but the wax image is more permanent than the 'scorched' image in Thermofax, and the costs are lower. A further variation—with perhaps more library possibilities—is to substitute for the dyed wax sheet a heat sensitive hectographic carbon behind the copy paper. In this way a reversed image is picked up on the back of the paper which can then be used as a master for hectographic (spirit) duplicating (see Chapter VI). It is difficult to achieve good quality, and hectographic duplicating itself spreads the image, but this method provides a useful link between photocopying and multiple reproduction processes. It is a poor quality equivalent of an electronic stencil for wax stencil duplicating, or platemaking by photocopy for small offset.

Dual spectrum overcomes the colour blindness of thermographic copying. The inability to reproduce from colours was recognised by the 3M company as a serious deficiency, and the first effort to overcome it was the issue of ball point pens with special ink which would reproduce. Of course this was of use only when the creation of the image was under the control of those who would copy it. The dual spectrum process was first introduced as a companion unit to the Thermofax copier: not only did it overcome colour blindness, but as the extra unit was flat-bed, books could be copied. Now dual spectrum is marketed as one integrated piece of equipment but it still suffers from the disadvantage of being two stage. The first exposure (not by infra-red light) produces an invisible (latent) image on a special intermediary sheet. This intermediary is fed into the heat copier to produce the final print. Quality is good, and although the exposure is two stage, there is no separate development, so not much delay is experienced in obtaining copies, and the process is dry and convenient. Dual spectrum would be a good buy for the very small library whose need of a photocopier is so slight and intermittent that the rental or purchase of an electrophotographic copier would not be justified.

Electrophotographic copying
The term 'electrophotographic' is now preferred by experts to 'electrostatic' by which name the process is still better known. There seems, indeed, very little reason for the change. It must be said at once that this kind of copying is near to eclipsing other photocopy methods except for special applications. A library buying its first photocopier today would almost certainly choose from the wide range of electrophotographic

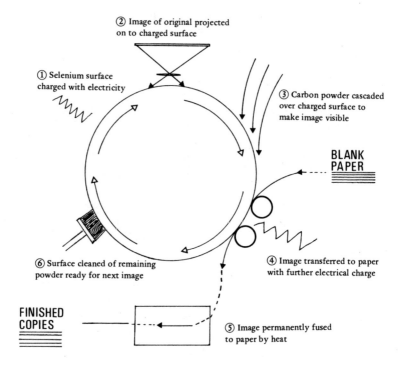

Fig 9 : Principle of automatic electrophotographic copying

models available. A rental system is common, but some are available for outright purchase. Even where present use does not seem to justify the expense compared with the lower initial costs of another process, demand will soon build up when the machine is installed because of its convenience. Whether that increased demand represents unwarranted and wasteful copying or better service to readers is a matter for the library to decide.

Before describing the equipment it is necessary to explain briefly the principles on which electrophotographic copying operates. The steps in making a copy are as follows, but it must be remembered that in present day copying the sequence is automatic and actuated by merely pressing a button.

1 An electric charge is given to a selenium surface which is on a metal backing. Selenium will not allow the charge to leak away to the metal while it is kept in the dark.

2 An image from the original to be copied is projected or reflected on to the selenium surface. The light from the non-text areas allows the electric charge to disperse to the metal, but the text being dark reflects no light and so the charge is held where the text falls on the selenium surface. Thus we have an invisible pattern of electric charges remaining in the shape of the text or other marks on the original.

3 To make the text visible carbon powder with an opposite electric charge is cascaded over the selenium surface. The powder sticks to the surface.

4 Paper is brought against the surface and by means of a further electric charge the powder is transferred to the paper.

5 The paper is heated to fuse the carbon to the paper. This bonds the image to the paper very securely, and carbon being a very stable substance, electrophotographic copies have the advantage of permanence.

Note that to explain the general principle simply, only one kind of electrophotographic process has been described. A variant, dealt with in more detail below, forms the copies not on a selenium surface for subsequent transfer, but on the copy paper itself. The copy paper is coated with a substance such as zinc oxide which acts in the same way as selenium.

The first electrophotographic equipment was not automatic. This was the Rank-Xerox VR (variable ratio) camera: basically a large camera, in principle like a Photostat or process camera in which the steps enumerated above were carried out separately with a good deal of handling by the operator. Selenium coated metal plates were employed. Such cameras were used not primarily to make copies on paper, but as a cheap and quick way to make good offset litho plates with the facility for enlargement and reduction. Some are still in use.

The first automatic copier was the Copyflo system, still much used, although production has ceased on this equipment. This is not a library or office copier, but apparatus for enlarging the whole of a microfilm on to a reel of paper at a speed of 20 feet per minute. (Other models are available to copy from a continuous flow of aperture cards or opaque originals such as cheques). The reel of paper from the microfilm version may be folded up and bound to give a somewhat crude but readable full-sized book. The bibliographical importance of this system is immense. The economics of microfilm and Copyflo are such that the production of one copy is perfectly feasible and, indeed, quite usual. Although this single copy will cost more than one would expect to pay for a copy conventionally produced from an edition of some thousands, it is astonishingly cheap in relation to its value. The slogan 'reprinting in an edition of one' is fully justified: Copyflo makes possible the reproduction of rare items, in single or few copies, where conventional methods, calling for an edition of some thousands to make them viable, would not be justified. It is possible, too, for the output of Copyflo to be lithographic master material, so that a larger number of copies can be produced without repeating the electrophotographic process for each one. In this way Copyflo can economically cater for the demand for a hundred or so copies and fill an obvious gap. Despite the cheapness of operation, Copyflo apparatus is extremely expensive to buy, and very few libraries have their own machines. Use is made of specialist companies such as Univeristy Microfilms on a service basis.

Office or library copiers work on the same principle as Copyflo—*ie* a continuous and automatic series of electrophotographic processes—but naturally they reproduce from hard copy instead of microfilm, and the copies are on separate sheets. It has already been mentioned that two versions of the technqiue of electrophotography are available—that using plain paper, and that using coated paper. Copying on to plain paper is the original Xerography, developed by the Xerox organisation, although other manufacturers have now entered this field. The coated paper version, sometimes known as Electrofax is marketed by very many companies. Here the copy is formed on the zinc oxide surface of the paper itself and not transferred on to plain paper from a selenium drum. The advantages of coated paper are that the reproduction of tone illustrations is sometimes better than is usual in Xerography, and that every copy is in effect a lithographic plate, so it can be used to obtain a hundred or so copies on a small offset machine. On the other hand some people find the shiny, rather tacky feel of the coated paper unpleasant, and ball point pen markings on the copy tend to bleach away.

The great popularity of electrophotographic copying means that there is a profusion of machines on the market. Sharing the same overall advantages of moderate cost per copy, speed and convenience, they compete with one another on the basis of price and the special features they offer. Some machines are available for outright sale at surprisingly low cost in view of the complexity of the engineering. It is probably volume production and the fact that development costs have now been paid off that allows this. The earliest Xerox automatic office copier—the 914—was obviously very expensive to develop and produce. To launch this new kind of copying successfully, some way had to be found to overcome the sales resistance of high initial cost, so the rental scheme was introduced. Most electrophotographic copiers—and some other equipment—are available for rental. For a fuller discussion of rental arrangements please see p21.

The library thinking of installing a copier has to choose between the different features offered by the various machines, all in relation to cost. It is exactly like buying a new car. Some features are useful to everyone, others are of particular value to some users. Coin operation, for example, will be looked for by college or other libraries whose policy is that readers shall pay directly for their copies. (The full economic cost need not necessarily be charged). Other users may have a need for tones to be well reproduced: some machines do better than others in this respect, and some have a special adjustment for light originals. Copiers which give various ratios of reduction of the original can be very useful in saving paper and reducing the expense of copying: for example if 10 copies are required of an A4 original 2 A5 copies can be made by reduction and then placed side by side on the machine for subsequent same-size production of 4 more copies, each bearing 2 half size images. Thus 10 readable if small prints are obtained for the price of only 6. The same facility can be used, at a lesser reduction, to convert the old foolscap size to the current A4. Other features of present day copiers are the ability to copy on both sides of the copy paper, and roll feed instead of the normal feed from sheets. This last advantage not only makes for economy, as a guillotine cuts off only the length of paper required for the particular image being reproduced, but it frees the machine from the trouble of paper jams which are not unknown in electrophotographic copiers and which sometimes constitute a fire risk.

'Xerox duplication' remains to be mentioned. Some electrophotographic machines are intended to be used for hundreds of copies from one original. This is the length of run for which one would expect to use a duplicator or small offset. In this system the copier is so metered that it charges a normal cost per copy for the first few prints from one original, but less if more copies are required. It will be seen from the explanation of the automatic electrophotographic process (p67) that the same cycle is repeated for every copy: there is no creation of a re-usable master as in duplicating proper. It is therefore inescapable that the true cost of the 100th copy is exactly the same as the cost of the first. The reduced charge for multiple copies is therefore no more than a marketing venture; a cut-back in profits to encourage increased use: a discount on quantity. True duplicating, with the cost of its cheap master spread over the number of copies produced must be cheaper in terms of materials. But there is a ready market for Xerox duplication and rightly so. It is convenient, it is speedy and so saves labour costs. It avoids the need for the installation of separate duplicating equipment and the bother of making a master. The quality it produces is often far higher than is possible in duplicating, and as a photocopy method it can reproduce anything on the original—letterheads, diagrams etc—without any master or plate-making techniques which could be costly, complicated, or unsatisfactory. Many libraries could therefore quite justifiably dispense with conventional duplicators, perhaps keeping small offset for longer run work.

CHAPTER VI

MULTIPLE REPRODUCTION

The term 'multiple reproduction' includes duplicating and small scale printing, usually by lithography, within the office or library. The name 'duplicating' might be stretched to cover all these processes, for small offset is most frequently used for simple jobs, but as pointed out in Chapter I it can also be employed for top quality work rivalling that of the professional printer.

We found it difficult to define reprography and felt it more useful to describe its characteristics instead. The same is true of multiple reproduction processes. The first characteristic divides these methods from photocopy in that runs of hundreds or even thousands of copies are typical. Secondly multiple reproduction depends on the creation of a master (a stencil or plate) from which copies are made on plain paper, *ie* paper with no light sensitive coating. Thus the principle is established at once, that in contrast to most photocopying, the more copies are produced, the cheaper the cost per individual copy. The cost of the paper is relatively low, and the expense of the master and its creation is spread between the number of copies made. The upper limit of the run is set by the durability of the master and the competition with faster and more sophisticated methods.

These characteristics may not satisfy everyone as a watertight working definition. Two apparent exceptions may be mentioned which seem to blur the distinction between photocopying and duplicating. At the end of the last chapter 'Xerox duplication' was discussed. This competes with duplicating and is specially marketed to do so, but is in fact photocopy artificially metered to give cheaper copies if many are required from one original. The nature of electrophotographic copying is to print on to plain paper, but no master is involved; the machine copies direct from the original, as in all photocopying. Were it not for the metering, which is purely a marketing venture, the cost of copies would not reduce with the number made. The other exception is dyeline photocopying which because of its cheapness can be used for more copies of one original than other photocopy methods. It may appear to be like a multiple reproduction process in that a master (a transparency) has to be used if the originals cannot be copied direct, but it remains photocopy as all copies must be on sensitized paper.

Hectographic duplicating

This is also known as spirit duplicating, also Banda, from the trade name of one of the leading manufacturers (in the same way that the proprietary name Photostat is loosely used of all photocopies).

The mechanics are simple. An image is typed, written or drawn on a sheet of plain glossy paper the back of which is in contact with a sheet of hectographic carbon. Thus a reverse image in carbon is picked up on the back of the master sheet. Duplication consists of bringing the carbon on the master in contact with the copy paper which has been moistened with alcohol. The spirit dissolves off enough of the carbon to give an image on each copy. An alternative method of master preparation is to use heat transfer photocopying (see Chapter V p65). This enables an already acceptable image (eg the page of a book) to be duplicated without retyping or other recreation of the image.

Different coloured carbons are available, but the commonly used purple is the strongest dye, and so gives the greatest number of copies. About 300 is the maximum for purple: much less, perhaps only 100, for the other colours. Because of this system of carbons hectographic duplicating has a unique advantage when copies in multiple colours are required—for example several graphs superimposed on the same axes. As many colours as are desired may be picked up on the same master sheet by replacing one coloured carbon with another. Therefore multi-colour work can be produced with only one pass through the duplicating machine, whereas other duplicating and printing processes must print each colour separately. Thus much time is saved and no 'register' problems of misalignment of one colour with another can arise.

Almost all hectographic machines are of a rotary type where the master is carried round a cylinder, but very simple flat-bed equipment intended for addressing envelopes is available, together with continuous stationery master material; this could have a use for catalogue card reproduction. The usual cylinder machines are either hand operated or electrically driven. Sophisticated models at the top end of the range are intended for 'systems' use in business and hardly concern the library, but one special feature, 'line selection', may be mentioned. Here it is possible not to print any given line or lines on the master by raising fingers of the damping pad so that they do not moisten the copy paper with spirit. Again this might be useful in the reproduction of catalogue entries where a selection could be made from alternative subject or other entry headings.

It must be admitted that hectographic duplicating does not give a high quality copy. The pressure and the dissolving of the dye on the master results in a little spreading of the image so that the sharpness and clarity of other processes is not possible. Also there is a risk of mess on the clothes and hands of operators from the strong dye of the carbon. Admittedly the carbon is protected by a plastic skin on the unused sheet, but mess is still possible when the skin is broken, either from the carbon sheet or the back of the master. The other disadvantage of the hecto-graphic method is that the image fades when exposed for a period to strong light, for example if left on a window sill. For many applications this does not matter, but some people prefer not to use it for permanent records such as catalogues even though their exposure to light will be minimal.

Nevertheless, hectographic duplicating stands up well to the competi-tion of higher quality processes. It is cheap—in machine cost and master material—and it is handy. Masters can be prepared easily not only by typing, but, in contrast to stencil duplicating, by handwriting and draw-ing. It is then, extremely useful for those numerous occasions when an informal internal note must be rushed out immediately with no time to go though the formal typing and reprographic channels.

There is scarcely room for three different multiple reproduction pro-cesses—hectographic, stencil and small offset—at least not in the same organisation. Small offset is in the ascendant: the process that will go to the wall is likely to be stencil, not hectographic duplicating.

Stencil duplicating
Like so many other processes, stencil or wax stencil duplicating is also known by the name of leading manufacturers, so giving them a free adver-tisement. 'To ronco' is a verb used in Britain, 'mimeographing' is used in the United States.

The principle is even simpler than that governing hectographic dupli-cating, and may be deduced from the name 'stencil'. The master consists of a thin sheet coated with a waxy substance impervious to ink. Typing (with no ribbon) or otherwise breaking through the wax skin by drawing etc allows ink to pass through on to the copy paper in the shape of the image. This is very similar, in fact, to silk screen printing.

The usual method of image creation is by typing. Wheel pens are available for ruling plain or patterned lines. Much less satisfactory results are obtained by writing or drawing with a pointed stylus as it is difficult to ensure that the wax is perfectly removed without damage to the thin carrier sheet. The result is that freehand work looks pale and weak, in contrast to the ease with which a hectographic (or offset) master can be prepared by manual methods. Several alternative master-making techniques are however available, alleviating the dependence on typescript. Thermographic copying can be used to prepare a stencil, also the duplicating companies run a service whereby ready made stencils can be prepared from the customer's own material at a moderate cost. An electronic stencil cutter can be purchased to make stencils from any acceptable copy, but the cost of the machine is as much, if not more, than the price of the duplicator itself.

Machines are almost always rotary with the stencil attached to the circumference of the drum or cylinder. The ink is within the drum and percolates through holes and felt to reach the stencil. Copy paper is brought against the stencil to receive an image. Machines can be operated by hand or electrically driven. Again there are simple flat bed methods which are designed for addressing but could be used for catalogue card reproduction. A small 'library card stencil' is also available for use on a rotary machine, but this requires either a specially small drum, or masking down the standard sized cylinder. There are sometimes problems, too, in keeping the flow of catalogue cards running straight through a rotary duplicator. As there are inevitable difficulties in matching the paper requirements of stencil duplicating with the kind of hardwearing card stock needed for catalogues, this method is not one of the best for catalogue card reproduction.

The paper requirement is a major drawback of stencil duplicating. In order that the ink may dry quickly enough to avoid marking ('setting off') on to the back of the following printed sheet, the paper must be absorbent enough for the ink to sink in at once. So the typical duplicating paper is not far removed from blotting paper—one can write on it with a ball-point but not a normal pen, it is neither pleasant to handle nor strong, and it picks up dirt easily. Moreover it is expensive. To some limited extent this drawback can be overcome. Better quality papers can be used in conjunction with resinous anti-set-off sprays to set the ink on the newly produced copy, or interleaving can be employed whereby sheets of absorbent paper are inserted between the copies as they are produced.

74

Or the machine can be run very slowly and each copy taken away to dry separately. The author remembers a cataloguing room where every shelf, ledge and window sill was covered with catalogue cards taking several days to dry completely. To use a more absorbent card would have resulted in a catalogue which would soon have become dog-eared through normal handling.

Stencil duplicating can be a good quality process. We have already noted the paper disadvantage and the difficulty of drawing or writing directly on a stencil. But for typescript material the image can be sharp and clean—much more so than in hectographic work. Where this is not achieved the fault probably lies in the operating rather than in the inherent faults of the process. Inking for example, is often insufficient and uneven, probably because operators do not bother to stop to re-ink where necessary. It is legitimate to mention this kind of fault; although it need not necessarily happen it is typical of much run-of-the-mill stencil duplicating. Add to this the very common shortcomings in design and image creation (discussed at the end of this chapter and in the next chapter) and one sees why so many duplicated documents are quite unnecessarily dreary and uninviting. On the other hand the copies produced in manufacturers' showrooms shows what can be done in stencil duplicating—quite passable tone illustrations, for example.

On many counts, stencil duplicating does not compete well with small offset. Offset is better in quality, more versatile, uses more acceptable paper, and can, if required, produce many more copies. Economics, too, favour small offset in most respects. The paper used is cheaper, and perhaps surprisingly, the short-run paper plate employed in litho printing is much cheaper than the duplicating stencil. Also, ink is taken up only where required in lithography; in stencil duplicating much ink is wasted in saturating all the felt, regardless of the amount of image. This is particularly true when a large drum is masked down. Thus the running costs all point in favour of small offset. Against this, one can say that stencil machines generally cost less than even the cheapest 'table top' offset equipment, and stencil duplicators are a little easier to use and maintain. They do not need the 'washing down' process to remove all the ink from the rollers which is a regular chore in small offset unless this is done by an automatic facility.

Small offset
'Small offset' describes the small lithographic printing machines used in libraries and offices. The principle of their operation is exactly the same as that used in large commercial lithographic printing establishments.

There the term 'offset printing' is used as a somewhat unhelpful shorthand for lithographic offset printing when the alternative 'litho' would be more descriptive. Where the plate is prepared by photography, as in the overwhelming preponderance of commercial work, the label 'photo-litho-offset' is appropriate. In small offset a trade name—Multilith—is often misused, as in other processes, to describe the method as a whole.

Any book on printing will describe the lithographic process. Suffice it to say here that the image on the master ('plate' is used in this context) must be in a grease-attracting substance in order to pick up ink, which is itself greasy. To stop ink sticking to the non-image areas of the plate, these areas are kept moist. As image and non image areas are in the same plane (in contrast to conventional letterpress printing) the two are kept apart merely by this well known principle of the mutual antipathy of grease and water.

Fig 10: The principle of offset printing

Perhaps the term 'offset' needs some explanation. The use of the offset principle is not necessarily confined to lithographic machines (there is now a development in the commercial printing world of letterpress offset) but its association with lithography has led, as we have mentioned, to the word being used as a handy tag for lithographic printing generally. All it means is that the plate prints not directly on to paper but on to the surface of another cylinder (called the offset blanket) and thence on to the paper. Diagram 10 shows the arrangement. There are several advantages of offset printing. One is that the plate lasts longer as it does not wear against the abrasive surface of the paper, but touches only the smooth rubber coating of the offset blanket. This surface being rubber is resilient, giving the advantage that it can impart the finest detail even when the paper is not entirely smooth. The effect is that the minute dots of a half tone illustration can be printed on normal text paper—there is no need for the unpleasant glossy art paper which is an expensive characteristic of illustrations in letterpress printed books. A further bonus of the offset principle affects small offset particularly, namely that the image on the plate can be the right way round. (The image on the offset blanket is therefore in reverse to print the right way round on the paper). So a small offset plate can be prepared by direct typing, drawing or writing, and provided the image is made in a greasy substance, it is as easy as making the same marks on an ordinary piece of paper.

It has been pointed out before (Chapter I) that small offset can be considered either as duplicating or as printing. It is both. While the majority of work done is of a type which could be handled by a stencil duplicator (though less well), the process is capable of a versatility, quality and run rivalling commercial printing. Even the simplest litho machine has the capacity for excellent results, but naturally enough there is a range of equipment available catering for the whole spectrum of quality, speed and specialised application which the market calls for. At the lowest end of the scale the simple table-top offset duplicator costs little more than a wax stencil machine. Higher in price come the faster running presses, and those taking a sheet size larger than the minimum foolscap or A4 which is by far the commonest size needed. Other features which can be obtained at a price are quick change of master and automatic wash-up. Automation is taken yet further in the case of 'total copy' or 'automatic duplicating' systems. Here the machine prints in sequence from a stack of masters; sometimes a platemaker is incorporated in the automatic process. When we come to two-colour machines and the like we are nearing the realm of the professional printer.

The masters or plates for offset litho display a similarly wide range catering for a variety of quality, cost and purpose. Thin metal plates are used for the longest runs—tens of thousands of copies if need be. Paper plates are for short run use and are very cheap—cheaper than the masters for stencil duplicating. Both paper and metal plates can receive their image either directly or by some plate making process. Direct methods are typing (with a greasy lithographic ribbon in the typewriter), drawing, writing or ruling lines with a special ballpoint, or painting etc for artistic effects. Provided greasy finger marks are kept off the surface, direct master preparation is almost as trouble free and easy as in the hectographic process. At the other end of the scale plates for the highest quality work—including full colour trichromatic printing—can be made by conventional photo-litho methods which the professional printer would use. Here a film negative, screened if necessary, is made in a process camera or by a scanner, then exposed to a light sensitive lithographic plate and subsequently developed. This somewhat lengthy process, using expensive equipment and materials, is commonly discarded in favour of some photocopy method of plate making which is a good compromise between quality, speed and convenience, and cost. Several photocopy systems are suitable, for example electrophotographic and chemical transfer. The simple machine used for paper copies can be employed, but special platemaking equipment is also available, sometimes giving the facility for size reduction on to the plate by use of a built-in camera. This enables typescript to be reduced in size to give a more handy page size and to resemble printed type more closely. We have already noted in Chapter V that coated paper copies from an electrophotographic copier will serve as short run masters. Also in Chapter II attention was drawn to the fact that plates can be made outside by the small offset manufacturing companies. This would be useful when the need for complicated high quality plates—for full colour work for example—is only occasional.

The low running cost means that small offset can be economic when perhaps as few as thirty copies are required. When litho's advantages in quality and versatility are added it can well be argued that there is no need for any institution to install a second duplicating method—hectographic or stencil—to back it up. Smaller numbers of copies, say up to fifty, can be conveniently obtained by Xerox duplication. But much depends on the immediate availability of copies from offset. If the printing is removed from the point of demand to a centralised reprographic unit as is common in small offset installations, there may be some administrative delays in getting work done. This is where well-sited push-button Xerox multiple copiers, with no need of master preparation, score. For maximum economy however, good access to quick copying can be obtained by providing simple hectographic duplicators which are suitable for direct use by staff and which are so distributed throughout the organisation that the formality of routing work through a centralised unit is avoided.

Ancillary equipment: binding
The methods described so far in this chapter can produce large quantities of paper which in many cases need some further processing—folding, collating, stapling, binding—before the product is ready for use. This is not always recognised: perhaps it is assumed that the output of duplicating is always a single sheet immediately ready for distribution. To avoid bottlenecks, therefore, consideration must be given to acquiring an appropriate range of ancillary equipment.

With much of the range little general guidance can be given as the need will vary greatly according to the type of work done. A guillotine is an obvious requirement, but whether or not there is a call for a folding machine will depend on the maximum size which can be printed. If it is A3, then folding down to A4 or A5 will be usual. If A4, most material may be needed in this size and if folded jobs are only occasionally wanted it might be done by hand. The necessity for a collator will very soon be felt, however. Tedious 'picking up' of sheets by hand to make a multi-sheet document can only be tolerated if the volume of this kind of work is very small. Labour costs would be high and the possibility of error great. A first buy could be a simple hand operated machine which jogs out a sheet for quick manual pick-up, but it is likely that an electrical collator will very soon be justified. Collators attached to duplicating machines—Xerox or small offset—are also available. These distribute the sheets as they are printed so that when all the pages have been duplicated the collation is complete at the same time.

Traditional binding methods suitable for full size books may be dismissed. The techniques at the disposal of the reprographic unit are wire staples, adhesive binding, spiral binding, and patent clips. Wire staples would probably be the first method to be employed by a small in-plant unit because everyone has a stapler and the various techniques are no more than a development of the universally used staple in the top left hand corner. Staplers are cheap and can be electrically operated. Two or more staplers can be ganged together. The simplest binding therefore is to staple two or three times down the spine edge. This *stabbing* method is secure provided the staples are long enough to give an adequate turn over on the back sheet. An alternative technique is to staple from front and back closely together and without clenching. This might be used

STABBING

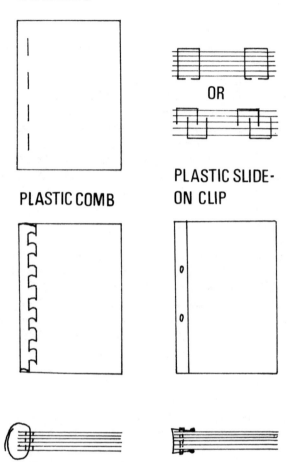

PLASTIC COMB

**PLASTIC SLIDE-
ON CLIP**

Fig 11: Some methods of binding (saddle stitching and unsewn binding are not illustrated)

where documents are thicker than the length of available staples. The disadvantage of both methods of stabbing is that the book is difficult to open and will not stay flat. Some of the print may be obscured unless generous inner margins have been allowed. The other stapling method can be used only on folded material. This is *saddle stitching*, so called from the shape of the inverted vee anvil on which the folded sheets are opened for stapling. Saddle stitching is very widely used in commercially produced pamphlets, brochures, etc, but there is a limit to the number of leaves which will fold and staple satisfactorily. There are no problems in opening the book, but the method shares the disadvantage of all wire stapling in that staples will rust in humid conditions, thus breaking, and discolouring pages. This is not likely to be a problem except where material is stored for a long time.

Adhesive or unsewn binding is also known as 'perfect' binding from an American trade name. It is widely used in commercial binding of new books, in tear-off pads and also sometimes in library rebinding where early failures in the technique made the term 'perfect' ironic. In this method an adhesive is brushed on the spine and penetrates a small distance between the leaves. A spine covering of mull (open weave muslin-like cloth) adds a little strength and holds more adhesive. Provided the book is not too heavy unsewn binding is of satisfactory strength. Equipment for in-plant use is extremely simple, consisting basically of adhesive, mull, and a clamp. Books bound in this way open well and look quite professional. This is a good and cheap method which could well be selected as the standard technique by any organisation.

Spiral or plastic comb binding originated in the commercial publishing world and was used for applications such as cookery books which need to open—and stay open—completely flat. At first a wire spiral, like a spring, was threaded through small circular holes punched near the spine edge of the leaves. Nowadays rectangular slots are punched and, in a special jig, a circular plastic 'comb' is opened out so that the spine can be inserted. When released the tongues on the comb penetrate the rectangular holes and the natural spring of the plastic material prevents their easy removal. If T-shaped slots are used pages can be added after binding. The equipment is more expensive than adhesive binding, but there is no danger of any messy working, and books open just as well or better. The binding is secure although there may be some danger of the first and last pages working loose after heavy use if they are not protected by card covers. Spirals tend to 'catch' in other books adjacent to them in shelving or filing, and some librarians may find it important that attaching a spine label bearing the class number etc is rarely satisfactory. Finally, various sizes and colours of plastic clips can be obtained which run the length of the spine, and which grip the leaves without penetrating them in any way. They are, alas, not very secure unless they have some special page locking device which does involve punching one or two holes through the leaves. The spine is gripped some little way in from the edge, so the book is difficult to open. Forcing the leaves apart will probably make the clip spring off, and it is remarkably difficult to re-insert the leaves, so some may be lost.

Design for in-plant printing

Whole books have been written about book design in general: this brief section makes no attempt to cover all of the same ground. Instead, some of the special problems of design for in-plant work are considered and some practical hints given. While the main process in mind is typewriter composed small offset much of the section will be relevant to hectographic and stencil duplicating although neither could really be described as in-plant printing. At the other end of the scale the advanced in-house printer, using photo composition and two colour presses will have such versatility in his expensive machinery that he will not experience the design constraints which are examined here.

We may first look at some of the widely accepted rules and conventions of layout. Some are valid both for commercial and in-plant work, some may need modification. Margins are an example of the need for adaptation. They are often inadequate in duplicated and small-offset productions, yet they are necessary not only for aesthetic appeal but for

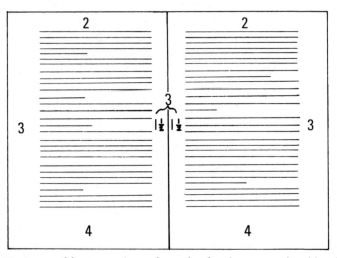

Fig 12: Acceptable proportions of margins for the conventional book. Modifications may be needed in in-plant work because of unjustified text and the need to give extra inner margins for some binding methods

practical usefulness. They must be sufficient to undergo cropping if the publication is ever rebound, a good margin enables the reader to hold the document without obscuring the text with the thumbs, and there is some evidence that the legibility of the print is enhanced by an adequate surround. The conventional view is that margins should take up about $\frac{3}{8}$ of the page area and might have proportions as follows: gutter (inner margin) $1\frac{1}{2}$; head 2; foredge 3; foot 4. Alternative proportions are 2, 3, 4 and 5 respectively. But with normal unjustified typescript the right hand margin is indefinite—a ragged edge makes nonsense of a precise margin calculation: this will apply to the outer (foredge) margin on the right hand page and the gutter margin on the left hand page. The narrow inner margin quoted in the proportions above presuppose two pages side by side to form an 'opening' of a book, thus the two adjacent gutter margins are seen as one unit. Naturally this does not apply if one is producing single sheets, although by convention the left hand margin in such cases is smaller than the right. A special allowance may have to be made in in-plant work for binding methods (such as wire stabbing or plastic clips) which take up some of the inner margin. As far as margins are concerned, therefore, the conventional rule should be taken as a guide but cannot be slavishly followed.

Much easier to follow is the accepted figure of 10-12 words as the maximum for any line of text if the eye is not to slip from line to line and thus slow up reading. There is no problem here in typescript, for with adequate margins, just about this average is achieved on an A4 sheet. On A5 it would be desirable to photo-reduce typescript, otherwise the very short lines may also slow reading because of the frequent moves from line to line. Reduced typescript may therefore be more legible for this reason, it looks more like type, and it can permit a page size which is handier and more acceptable because of its similarity to the conventional book. Where for some reason lines have to be overlong, it is more than ever necessary to have adequate inter-linear spacing to reduce reading strain. A page of text can also be made more inviting—for psychological rather than optical reasons—by breaking up the solid panel of text by avoidance of overlong paragraphs, and by the insertion of headings, diagrams etc in the text.

Because of the limitations of the typical equipment, in-plant printing has special problems not shared by the producer of the conventional book. We have already mentioned the fixed size of unreduced typescript. It is also easier to produce poor quality work if proper care is not taken—the weak inking in stencil duplicating is an example. But even if he is prepared to use his equipment properly, the in-plant printer will try to avoid needless work which could prove troublesome on the simplest machines. Multi-colour jobs for instance involve more than one pass through the press, with attendant problems of register. They therefore cause more work, time and expense, and have a higher risk of wastage. Certainly such devices as coloured headings are desirable in giving greater variation and impact, but many will look for easier alternatives. One of these is to use coloured paper. The interest of colour is retained, the opacity of the paper is improved, and a useful bonus is the facility of distinguishing by a colour coding between the various parts of a publication.

An inherent drawback of using a typewriter to create text is that this method lacks the typographical variation possible by using printer's type. Metal type (or filmsetting) offers differences in type faces and weights, a range of sizes, and useful variants such as italic and small capitals. Some of these features can be matched by some typewriters, as will be demonstrated in the next chapter, but most reprographic work is typed on a fairly standard typewriter without refinements. The in-plant printer must therefore use other means such as the clever use of spacing to make up for his lack of typographic flexibility. Indentation and generous blanks can distinguish one section of text from another, while the problem of making a clear hierarchy of headings can be solved by resorting to letterspacing, underlining, variations of capitals and lower case letters, and alternating between centred headings and those ranged to the left.

Variation in headings ceases to be a problem if a headlining method is used for them instead of typescript. These methods are described in Chapter VII on 'Creating the image'. The same is true for covers of publications if these are to catch the eye with large lettering and possibly the use of colour. The extra work involved in using non-typing methods to produce a striking cover may hardly be justified if the run is short, but a good way out of the difficulty is to produce a large stock of covers which can be adapted to different publications. These could be printed professionally as an outside job. Thus all issues of a new books bulletin would have the same standard cover, but could be overprinted with the date of the particular issue. An alternative to overprinting is to have a hole cut in the cover or a corner snipped off, so that the title or date of the individual document, printed on the first sheet, shows through. In this way economy and the impact of a professional-looking cover are combined.

Having overcome, as best he can, the limitations of his medium, the in-plant printer still has to make aesthetic judgements about design, particularly in relation to covers and main headings of single page news sheets, book-lists etc. These judgements depend on flair and experience and cannot easily be taught, but some hints may be appropriate. A general guiding principle should be simplicity. If different type styles are available it is better not to mix them in one piece of printing. Similarly, unless real confidence has been built up, it is unwise to mix both centred and ranged-to-left material on one cover or title page (as distinct from headings in the text mentioned earlier). There is a natural urge in all designers to try to be different, but it can lead to disaster in inexperienced hands. Examples are printing running diagonally across the page, or, worse, letters set one below the other vertically, which destroys the normal word patterns which are the basis of reading. The tiresome habit of eschewing all capitals is beloved by some, but it is very passé and reminds one of the worst self-conscious design of the 1930's. On the other hand, weak designers use block capitals far too much, in the mistaken belief that they are more emphatic than lower case. In fact the reverse is true: a large size of lower case has more impact and is more legible than capitals as the individual shape of a word is immediately recognisable from the pattern of the ascenders and descenders. Motorway signs have demonstrated this phenomenon.

The purpose of a cover design or display heading of a news sheet is to attract attention by its visual appeal and to communicate not only the title of the document but its source. So an image of the library or information unit is built up. This build up of image can be greatly helped by a consistent 'house style' which becomes immediately recognisable as belonging to the library or a particular publication. House style could comprise the use of one display typeface for the title, layout, a distinctive colour, or a combination of these features and others. A useful and commonly employed device is a 'logo'—usually the name or initials of an organisation set in a special way, often with letters intertwined. (See the publisher's logo on the spine of this book). More impact is achieved if this is in reverse form, with the letters in white against an inked patch which could be regular or irregular in shape. The amount of ink, whether black or colour, makes this reversed kind of symbol more arresting. Such a logo once made can of course be photocopied for re use wherever required and it would be worthwhile to get it set up professionally by an outside printer. A further benefit of a consistent house style is that it reduces the work of re-design for each individual production and saves the need for different instructions to operators.

Finally, a brief mention must be made of editorial requirements relating to the content of printed documents, although strictly speaking they are outside the scope of this book. Some in-plant work is not properly paginated for example, and date of publication is frequently omitted. Librarians would expect proper citations to be given in references, booklists, etc, and in the case of the kind of material under discussion in this chapter which is not issued by well known publishers, it is important to give not only the publisher's name, but his address, if acquisitions librarians are not to be frustrated.

CHAPTER VII

CREATING THE IMAGE

Some of the reproduction methods discussed in this book—particularly small offset described in the last chapter—are capable of a quality rivalling that of the professional printer. The most widespread limitation of in-plant work is image creation: it is this above all which makes reprography look amateur compared with commercial print. While the good in-plant job can be well produced in regard to layout, presswork and binding, it usually suffers in that the text is composed on a typewriter which lacks the wide variety of weights, sizes and styles which are available in printer's type. Headings and covers also pose a special problem.

This chapter therefore concentrates on these two areas of typewriters and larger display lettering. These image creation methods will be used largely for multiple reproduction processes, but they will apply in all cases, including microcopy and photocopy, where the image is originated within the organisation and is not merely taken from, say, a periodical article already set up in type. But in passing it should be mentioned that there are more methods of image creation than are dealt with in this chapter. We have already referred to indirect methods; ie the transfer of an already acceptable image on to a master for subsequent reproduction. Direct methods include handwriting, drawing, ruling lines etc as well as typing, but do not need any further explanation. We have considered that filmsetting text composition systems are outside the scope of this book. Tone illustrations, often a difficulty throughout reprography, require, for best results, a screen incorporated in the photographic process to break the image up into printable dots, or the newer alternative of a scanning machine which by-passes the photographic stage.

It is worth putting effort into methods of making the original image, and not only on grounds of quality. The process in inherently expensive, as it necessarily involves much labour cost; it is absurd therefore to spend much money to achieve a poor result when little or no extra expenditure would improve quality markedly. The major part of the cost of many reprographic jobs is represented by the image creation, not the reproduction. Even the simplest typing can be remarkably costly. This can be demonstrated by dividing a typist's daily wage by the number of usable typed sheets she produces in this time. Account must be taken of waiting and wasted time and the time taken to do corrections, set up the typewriter and stationery, etc. Original image making always implies checking, usually by someone more highly paid than the typist. So again it must be stressed that it is wasteful folly to create an image of any one original more than once. If that which is to be reproduced is acceptable as it stands it should be transferred on to a master by photocopying etc rather than retyping. And once a typing is done, every effort should be made to avoid the need to repeat it, even for another format.

For maximum quality and economy there is a need for good equipment and good operating staff. This chapter illustrates for example, how some relatively inexpensive typewriters have features which are important in achieving high standards. Of course, maintenance and cleaning of machines is vital; even the best machine produces poor work if the type is dirty or the mechanism ill adjusted. Most crucial of all is the quality of staff. An inefficient typist is not paid much less than a very good one, but her real cost may be much higher because of her slowness and her greater proportion of unacceptable and therefore wasted work. She will spend much more time on corrections, and will not have the ability to produce a good layout without repeated—and often vain—instructions.

Typewriters—features

Typewriting intended for subsequent reprographic reproduction is usually known as *repro-typing* to distinguish it from ordinary typing used for correspondence etc. Any typewriter can be used, but for best results machines with certain special features may be employed. These features are by no means always expensive and unusual; indeed a typewriter suitable for reprographic work is quite often no more than a machine commonly used by many organisations for correspondence. There is therefore a considerable overlap between repro- and ordinary typing. Since most equipment can be thought of as dual-purpose, the small library with only intermittent reprographic needs should not feel inhibited in buying a typewriter which will serve well for reprographic purposes.

Electrical action is an example of this. Electric typewriters are widely used for general typing, but they are particularly important in reprographic image creation. Obviously the image must be even in density;

a skilled manual typist may achieve this, an electric typewriter certainly does. Manufacturers claim 20% more productivity for electrical action, but one would not often reach this figure except by direct comparison over long pieces of work. A further bonus is the 'repeat button' which enables underlinings to be done, for example, without repeatedly hammering at a key. Typists take a little time to adjust to the touch of an electric typewriter: it is disconcerting that the slightest touch of a key—perhaps in error—is rewarded by a character at full force. The claimed advantage of being able to produce up to twenty carbon copies at one typing proves to be unsubstantial and is certainly an inefficient and expensive way of making multiple copies. Not only are the copies progressively more faint and unsharp, but the labour of collating and decollating carbons, and making corrections on the individual copies, is considerable.

The image reaches the paper from the typewriter normally through an inked ribbon. This is re-usable, so towards the end of its life characters appear as grey rather than black. Moreover the fabric pattern of the ribbon causes an unsharpness at the edges of the letters. These drawbacks can be overcome by using a non re-usable ribbon on a paper or plastic base. Here every character is uniformly and intensely black as it receives pigment from a fresh ribbon. The edges are sharp as there is no fabric pattern.

Ordinary typescript falls short of the professional appearance of printer's type in three major respects: the crude and monotonous typeface commonly employed; the lack of proportional spacing; and the lack of justification of the lines. All of these can be remedied, the first two by quite inexpensive typewriters, the last by a greater expenditure of time and money (and we will question later whether justification is worth the effort).

Typewriters are widely available with one of a range of different faces, most of which resemble professional print quite closely, certainly more than normal typescript. They are often called 'shaded faces' because, like type, letters have a contrast between thick and thin strokes. (In ordinary typescript the letters are 'monotone' ie the stems are the same thickness throughout). The appearance of the work is vastly enhanced by the use of these machines, but note that typefaces are not interchangeable; the choice of one fixed face is made when the typewriter is purchased. Some nod towards interchangeability is made by one device which enables a single character to be interchanged on one key, and another device allows a thickened or 'bold face' character to be produced by typing twice with a slight displacement of the carriage.

Fig 13: Typescript

The major differences between the appearance of ordinary typescript and printer's type are that the former (a) employs an uninteresting 'monotone' face, (b) gives each character the same lateral space, distorting the natural varied width of letters, and (c) leaves a ragged or 'unjustified' right hand edge to the page. But these disadvantages can be overcome. Proportional spacing and a variety of handsome typefaces are available on relatively inexpensive typewriters. A justifying typewriter costs much more, and usually two typings are required. Justification is a hangover from letterpress printing: is it worth it?

Ordinary typescript

The major differences between the appearance of ordinary typescript and printers' type are that the former (a) employs an uninteresting 'monotone' face, (b) gives each character the same lateral space, distorting the natural varied width of letters, and (c) leaves a ragged or 'unjustified' right hand edge to the page. But these disadvantages can be overcome. Proportional spacing and a variety of handsome typefaces are available on relatively inexpensive typewriters. A justifying typewriter costs more, and usually two typings are required. Justification is a hangover from letterpress printing: is it worth it?

Type face like printer's type and proportional spacing (IBM Executive)

The major differences between the appearance of ordinary typescript and printer's type are that the former (a) employs an uninteresting 'monotone' face, (b) gives each character the same lateral space, distorting the natural varied width of letters, and (c) leaves a ragged or 'unjustified' right hand edge to the page. But these disadvantages can be overcome. Proportional spacing and a variety of handsome typefaces are available on relatively inexpensive typewriters. A justifying typewriter costs much more, and usually two typings are required. Justification is a hangover from letterpress printing: is it worth it?

Justified text (IBM Composer)

Fully interchangeable typeface systems were the province of the Varityper machines until the IBM 72 range was introduced. The cheapest of the latter brings interchangeability down to near the cost of an ordinary electric typewriter, without, at this price, the facilities for proportional spacing and justification. The IBM 72 is familiarly known as the 'golf ball' typewriter from the shape of the interchangeable type-head. The

Varityper machines (which also justify) have rather more expensive curved type elements. Both systems have a wide range of faces from which to choose.

Proportional spacing recognises the different widths of characters, which ordinary typing does not. So where there is a lack of proportional spacing, as is common, a letter 'm' is cruelly compressed and a letter 'i' unduly extended so that they both occupy the same width. The reason is simply that for ease of construction the carriage moves along the same standard distance for each character struck. In proportional spacing typewriters the carriage moves a distance appropriate to the width of the characters—a more complicated engineering feat. But letters look 'right', much more like print, and appearance is much improved. The only snag is correction: if one has mistyped an 'i' instead of an 'm' there will be in-sufficient space to insert the right letter. Proportional spacing is not necessarily expensive: it is available on the non-interchangeable 'shaded face' typewriters referred to above. Clearly however, the engineering problems become more complex if proportional spacing is applied to a typewriter which also offers interchangeable type or aid in justification; in the former there would be different widths of characters for each typeface used. The combination of proportional spacing with these other features is certainly possible, but one climbs steeply up the price range to find it.

Justifying typewriters—typewriter composition
So far we have mainly considered typewriters which are inexpensive enough to be well within the range of libraries and information units with the need for only a modest reprographic service, and no wish to spend much more than the cost of an ordinary typewriter. With justifying type-writers we enter a new range: the cheapest are at least three times as ex-pensive as the simple typewriters first described in this chapter, or approaching the cost of a baby-sized European car. The upper end of this range—represented by both IBM and Varityper models—cope with proportional spacing as well as interchangeability of typeface and justi-fication and are three times more expensive again. In car terms we are at the bigger than average family model, or sports car price bracket. Earlier in this chapter we introduced the term 'repro-typing' to distinguish from typing for general correspondence purposes; at the level of complex ity we have now reached we can now describe the process as *typewriter composition*. Some of the machines, such as the IBM 72 Composer,

indicate this by their name. As before, the definition overlaps with the simpler repro-typing already dealt with. Typewriter composition is capable of such quality that it deserves this title: it is a reasonable and cheap substitute for the conventional methods of composition, either in metal as for letterpress printing or filmsetting (photosetting) often used with lithography. For this reason typewriter composition is not only used for in-plant printing, *eg* by small offset. Some commercial publishers are reducing their costs in this way, although, of course, the printing will be on full sized lithographic presses, and binding will not be confined to the do-it-yourself methods described in the last chapter. This book is produced in this way.

Justifying text—*ie* making all lines equal in length as in print—not only involves the expense of purchasing a special typewriter, but as we shall see later, usually does not avoid the necessity of typing twice, so labour costs are increased. It may well be questioned whether justification is worth the extra cost and trouble. Justified text is familiar to readers from the conventional letterpress produced book and so they have come to expect it, but outside letterpress there is no functional reason for it. In metal type there is a real need for all four edges of a page of type to be solid and straight lines: a ragged right hand edge would crumble into disarray when the type for a page was moved around during imposition and make-up of the formes. (It would be possible to fill out all lines exactly with spaces, but this would be almost the same trouble as inserting the extra spaces between the words and so justifying the line). Typewriter composition, and filmsetting too, not being three dimensional as is type, are not hampered by this restraint; unjustified text causes no trouble at all (except perhaps in the exact calculation of margins—see Chapter VI p82). But tradition dies particularly hard in the world of the printed word, and so there is a demand for justification. There are some signs that the tradition is breaking down, even in conventionally printed work which has full facilities for justification, perhaps merely as a design fad. Also the purist could claim that *any* justification distorts the proper inter-word spaces. These points could be made when countering the insistence by others that in-plant produced material must look exactly like 'real books'. Whether or not a justifying system is installed may in fact depend on the expectations, even the demands, of the users of the work produced. Indeed the success of a proposal to establish in-plant production as an alternative to putting work outside may hinge on convincing some high-level decision maker that typewriter composition can do everything the printer can.

To explain the mechanics of justification we may look at the ludicrous situation of attempting to justify with an ordinary typewriter. It is theoretically possible, but it would be slow and tedious in the extreme. The line would be typed and the number of characters counted. Obviously the line would not, except by remote chance, fill the desired length of line exactly—there would be a few spaces left over at the end. These spare spaces would then be divided up and put into the inter-word spaces on the second typing so that when complete the line would be at the full standard length with somewhat increased spaces between the words. If there are (say) 3 extra spaces and 5 word breaks then clearly the inter-word spacing will be uneven on the second typing, but a typewriter with a half spacing facility will give extra flexibility. Justifying typewriters such as Varitypers have this fine adjustment for spacing, but their essential characteristic is that they merely relieve the operator of the chore of counting characters and spaces. It is still necessary to type twice—first for the input to the machine's calculator, and second to produce the final justified line. Although universally known as justifying typewriters they are only *aids* to justification. Particularly when combined with proportional spacing, they are, as indicated, expensive.

There are non-retyping methods. One is a special version of the tape operated typewriter where one machine produces a tape which is then fed into a second machine which automatically types justified copy. In other words the second typing is automatic, and the principle is rather similar to that which governs a Monotype hot metal composing machine—or some filmsetters. The cost, too, is comparable to some of the smaller filmsetters, and to pursue our comparison with car prices, we are now at the Rolls Royce level. Other attempts to solve the justification problem have included typing on to special stretchable paper; typed lines are lifted from the backing sheet, extended to their proper length and re-placed. An optical system can do the same thing, *ie* lines of typescript can be optically stretched and re-photographed, and a slanting can be incorporated to give italics. Note that here the characters themselves are extended but the small distortion is acceptable unless lines are very short for the measure. These optical systems are again bringing us into the techniques and cost area of text filmsetting which would certainly be considered by the large in-plant unit. They are, however, beyond the scope of this book.

Large lettering for headings and covers
This chapter indicates how high quality text can be produced by typewriters, but the problem of larger sizes of lettering, needed for headings

or covers, remains. It is not quite true that all typewriters are unsuitable for this purpose as a few 'bulletin typewriters' are available with a very large face, but obviously the typography is extremely restricted. Another method which may be briefly dismissed is the handwriting of headings and freehand drawing of cover design. The appearance is appallingly amateur unless someone in the organisation has very special calligraphic and design skills.

At the end of the last section reference was made to filmsetting as beyond the range of equipment which this book covers. This is true of photocomposition for text setting, but not true of small hand operated

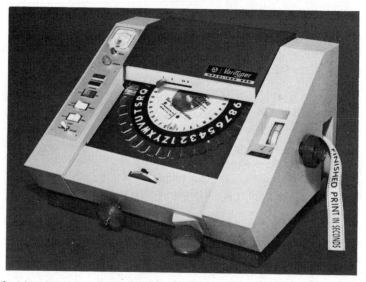

Fig 14: AM Varityper Model 820 Headliner. The 'dialling' system referred to in the text

systems for setting a line or two of display work. These machines are quite cheap and basically consist of no more than a photographic enlarger which prints out slowly, letter by letter, on to a strip of photographic paper which may then be suitably arranged for a cover, or stuck into the appropriate place in the text for a heading. The 'negative' in the enlarger is a length of film bearing an alphabet; many different type styles are available. Manual positioning and re-positioning of the negative is required in some machines, but others are automatically operated. One,

94

for example, is reminiscent of the coin-operated machines found on railway stations which produce a name or other short text on a strip of aluminium; in the headlining machine the letters are similarly dialled in sequence.

The other major headlining and cover technique is the use of pressure-adhesive letters. There are many brands and varieties, but one of the leading names is Letraset. Sheets of alphabets are available in an extremely wide range of type faces and sizes. Tints and conventional symbols can also be obtained. Pressure by rubbing on the front of the required character releases it from its carrier sheet and affixes it where wanted on the paper beneath. The Letraset system involves no capital cost at all— merely the running cost of providing and replacing the alphabet sheets. Naturally there is some wastage as some letters of the alphabet will be expended before others leaving unusable characters on heavily used sheets. Wastage may also come from faulty technique; being an entirely hand operated method some care in spacing of letters and alignment of the lines is needed. It is somewhat slow. But with no machine to buy it is an eminently suitable way for the small user to introduce a wide variety of type styles into his work. If the order to the manufacturer is sufficient, special sheets can be made up to the customer's design; it could be very useful for example to have in this way professionally made supplies of the organisation's 'logo' or name style. (see Chapter VI p85).

Finally the large in-plant unit with a constant need to produce a variety of covers etc might find it justified to invest in a range of printer's type and a small letterpress printing press. While full letterpress text composition by machine would be quite outside the economics of reprography, the small amount of hand setting involved in display work could well be feasible.

CHAPTER VIII

INFORMATION SOURCES

This is an elementary book and some of its readers may wish to pursue the subject further. Those who are nearing the point of purchase of equipment will certainly need much more detailed information than is contained in the previous chapters and will need to ensure that it is completely up to date. Such information can be obtained from three main sources, namely published material, advice from expert independent organisations, and data from manufacturers.

An exhaustive list of these sources is hardly feasible. A complete book list on reprography for example (to say nothing of periodical articles) would take up much space, not altogether usefully, as the majority of the literature is in series produced by various organisations. It may be more helpful, therefore, to give a brief account of some of the major bodies in the field, with indicative references to some of the titles they publish. In this way bibliographical and other information can easily be updated by an enquiry to the organisation concerned. A list of their addresses is appended. A further list gives manufacturers of equipment, with brief notes on the type of product they offer. No addresses are given here as they can be found in directories in the countries concerned. The list is confined to major international companies for obvious practical reasons. There are many local suppliers, and it should be noted that some reprographic equipment, especially electrophotographic office copiers, is marketed through office supply firms.

Organisations and their publications
Pride of place should go to the National Reprographic Centre for documentation, not only because of the help given—directly and indirectly— in the preparation of this book. This is an important British centre of research into reprography and evaluation of equipment. Brief enquiries are answered free to subscribers: a small charge may be made to non-members. The centre also has a teaching function. There is a full programme of

courses, usually of a week's duration, and about two per year are specifically intended for librarians. Excellent brief course notes are provided. Other publications include a large number of evaluation reports on specific items of reprographic equipment: two more general titles in this series are *Microform reader/printers for libraries: a survey* (TER 73/1, 1973) and *Microfilm readers: a review of the trends* (TER 73/4, 1973). Librarians wishing to place work outside the library may wish to see *Directory of commercial microfilm services in the UK* (3rd ed 1974) while many will be interested in J R Spencer's *An appraisal of Computer Output Microfilm for library catalogues* (1974). COM cataloguing is also the subject of two of the titles in the occasional papers series. The NRCd was joint publisher (with the Library Association) of B J S Williams's important *Miniaturised communications: a review of microforms* (1970). The centre's journals are *NRCd bulletin* and *Reprographics quarterly*, which include abstracts.

The professional body covering the whole field of reprography in Britain is the Institute of Reprographic Technology. It organises national seminars on various topics and conducts evening meetings in the local regions into which it is divided. Qualifications in reprography are awarded by examination or the submission of a paper, but the highest rank of fellowship is gained through election by the council. Publications include a bulletin and a series of textbooks under the general title 'The reprographic library'. None are specifically aimed at librarians, though *Typewriting and office duplicating processes* by A W Gardiner (Focal Press 1968) may be mentioned. Note that the institute's books are issued in association with a commercial publisher. The latest publication is F C Crix's *Reprographic management handbook* (Business Books 1975) with a content wider than the title suggests. The international body responsible for reprography and recognised as such by Unesco is the International Council for Reprography. One of its major activities is to organise the International Congress for Reprography every three years.

Librarians will naturally turn to their own professional sources for information as clearly any advice and publications will be usefully biased towards library needs. So *Library and information science abstracts* (Library Association), *Library literature* (H W Wilson Co) and *Information science abstracts* (Documentation Abstracts Inc) will be searched for periodical articles. The American Library Association's Library Technology Program has produced several reports in the field of reprography. Most of the matter of the earlier works was incorporated into W R Hawken's *Copying methods manual* (LTP Publication No 11, 1966) but *Catalogue card reproduction* (LTP Publication No 9, 1965) should be seen if a very detailed account of this topic, with full costings, is required. A continuing series of Library Technology Reports evaluates particular models of equipment.

The (British) Library Association has nothing as ambitious as the Library Technology Program but its interest in reprography for librarians can be demonstrated. It was concerned in the formation of the Microfilm Association of Great Britain, and is joint publisher, with NRCd, of Williams's book referred to above. Other Library Association publications on reprography are old and out of print, but it would be worth while to seek out a copy of P S Pargeter's *Reproduction of catalogue entries* (LA Pamphlet No 20, 1960) for a clear and brief account of a topic which does not date too much. The forthcoming volume *British librarianship and information science 1970-1975* (due 1976) should include a documented chapter on developments in reprography.

Archive work—a sister profession to librarianship—is catered for by A H Leisinger's *Microphotography for archives* published in 1968 by the International Council on Archives.

The Association of Assistant Librarians—a group of the Library Association—published in 1968 D Mason's *Document reproduction in libraries*, the book referred to in the preface as covering the same ground as the present volume. In fact the two books are complementary in many respects: the approaches are different. Mason includes much material not found here and *vice versa*. He has chapters on bibliographical control, on the management of a reprographic unit, and a detailed account of the British copyright regulations. Inevitably the whole book is now a little dated, but it must be said that the chapter on photocopying was seriously out of date when it was written.

There is a separate network of organisations in the field of microforms, even though microtechniques are within the purview of the general reprographic bodies. There is therefore an unfortunate overlap, and it might be hoped that the Institute of Reprographic Technology and the Microfilm Association of Great Britain, for example, might see fit to merge at some time in the future. If the interest of the MAGB can be differentiated from that of the IRT it is probably on the grounds that it is more concerned with promoting the use of microforms and a little less with the technicalities. MAGB publications include the quarterly *Microdoc*, reports of seminars such as *COM applications in libraries* (1974) and *A directory of British photoreproduction services for libraries* (1974).

The USA equivalent of MAGB is the National Microfilm Association; their publications are obtainable in the UK through MAGB at a reduced price to members of the British association. These range from very brief guides such as *Introduction to micrographics* (1973) and *How to select a reader or reader/printer* (1974) to the 800 page *Guide to microreproduction equipment* (5th ed 1971) with its supplements. The world body in the field of microfilm is the International Micrographic Congress, publishers of *International directory of micrographic equipment* (ed J Rubin, 1967) which deals with countries outside the USA and so supplements the work cited immediately above. The quarterly *IMC journal* is sent free to members of MAGB. Another international organisation, but confined to one format, is the Microfiche Foundation. Its *Newsletter* appears three or four times a year: other publications include *Microfiche services in libraries* (2nd 1969) by J H I de Bruin and C Sobey. The *Microfiche bibliography* is to be discontinued.

A special type of information source is the consultant. Mention must be made of the firm of microfilm consultants, G G Baker and Associates, not only because they are the British agents for the standards issued by National Microfilm Association of America, but because of their range of up-to-date publications. These are frequently revised or updated by supplements. Examples are: *A guide to COM in the UK* (4th ed 1975); *A guide to the production of microforms* (1974) and *A guide to microfilm readers and reader/printers* (1974). These up-to-the-minute guides describe the range of equipment currently available and would be invaluable to librarians about to make a purchase. Sets of colour slides and lecture notes are also available.

A guide not only to available equipment, but to material published in microform, comes, appropriately enough, as a set of fiches, with hard copy indexes. This is the *International file of microfilm publications and equipment* (1974) edited by R B Selwyn of University Microfilms. (UK address: St John's Road, Tyler's Green, High Wycombe, Buckinghamshire). It is intended to revise and re-issue the whole annually.

Finally, the obvious point must be made that some books on reprography are produced by commercial publishers and other organisations which are not themselves within the reprographic or librarianship worlds. This is understandable in view of the wide applicability of reprography: as we have said earlier in this book the markets in business and industry are far greater than those in libraries. Sometimes, however, the publisher has a kindred interest, as with Business Books. This company produced *Copying, duplication and microfilm* by H T Chambers (1970) before its association with the IRT publishing programme noted above. Similarly, it is not surprising that Focal Press, photographic handbook specialists and the previous collaborator with IRT publishing, should have issued *Microcopying methods* by the late H R Verry (2nd edition revised by G H Wright, 1967). From the rest perhaps one excellent brief guide could be singled out. This is S B Page's *Modern office copying: photocopying, duplicating and near print* (Deutsch 1966). The author, a librarian, writes in a characteristic Australian no-nonsense style: his book has humour as well as clarity.

Addresses of the organisations cited

American Library Association
50 East Huron Street, Chicago, Illinois 60611 (USA)

GG Baker and Associates
54 Quarry Street, Guildford, Surrey GU1 3UF (UK)

International Council for Reprography
Secretary General: T Hampshire FIRT
National Reprographic Centre for documentation,
Hatfield Polytechnic, Endymion Road Annexe, Hatfield, Hertfordshire AL10 8AU (UK)

International Council on Archives
60 Rue des Francs-Bourgeois, Paris 75003 (France)

International Micrographic Congress
P O Box 484, Delmar, California (USA)

Institute of Reprographic Technology
52-55 Carnaby Street, London W1V 1PF (UK)

Library Association
7 Ridgmount Street, Store Street, London WC1E 7AE (UK)

Microfiche Foundation
101 Doelenstraat, Delft (Netherlands)

Microfilm Association of Great Britain
1 & 2 Trinity Churchyard, High Street, Guildford, Surrey GU1 3RW (UK)

National Microfilm Association
Suite 1101, 8728 Colesville Road, Silver Spring, Maryland 20910 (USA)

National Reprographic Centre for documentation
Hatfield Polytechnic, Endymion Road Annexe,
Hatfield, Hertfordshire AL10 8AU (UK)

Brief list of international manufacturers and suppliers

Notes: The designation 'Ltd', 'Inc' etc is ommitted as this will vary between countries.

The information is set out in the following order:

1 NAME followed by variants and initials if commonly used.
2 Whether company markets abroad through international branches bearing its own name, or through variously named agencies.
3 Trade names other than the name of the company.
4 Type of product supplied.

ADDRESSOGRAPH-MULTIGRAPH (AM)
International branches or NCR
Trade names: BRUNING MULTILITH VARITYPER
Electrophotographic copying. Typewriter composition and headline machines. Small offset and ancillaries.

AGFA-GEVAERT
International branches or agents
Photographic and electrophotographic copying. Microforms.

APECO
Agents
Electrophotographic copying.

BELL AND HOWELL
International branches or agents
Microforms: cameras, readers and processing.

CAPS MICROFILM
Agents
Microforms

DATAGRAPHIX
International branches
COM equipment.

A B DICK
International branches or agents
Trade name: MIMEOGRAPH
Stencil duplicating. Small offset. Electrophotographic copying.

FUJI
International branches or agents
Microforms

GAF
International branches
Diazo. Microforms.

GESTETNER
International branches or agents
Trade names: GESTEFAX GESTELITH
Stencil duplicating (including electronic stencil cutter). Small offset.

ILFORD
International branches or agents
Photographic copying. Film manufacturers.

IMAGE SYSTEMS
International branches
Microform readers and retrieval devices.

INTERNATIONAL BUSINESS MACHINES (IBM)
International branches
Typewriters for repro-typing and typewriter composition. Electrophoto-
graphic copying.

KALLE
International branches or agents (sometimes Hoerst Chemicals)
Diazo. Small offset supplies. Electrophotographic copying.

KODAK
International branches or agents
Trade names: EKTALITH INSTAFAX VERILITH
Photographic (diffusion transfer) copying. Microforms.

MEMOREX
International branches
Microforms. COM equipment.

MICROBOX
International branches and agents
Microforms.

MINNESOTA MINING AND MANUFACTURING COMPANY (3M)
International branches
Trade names: FILMAC THERMOFAX
Thermographic copying (including dual spectrum)
Offset litho supplies (eg, plates and platemakers)
Microforms.

NASHUA-COPYCAT
International branches or agents
Electrophotographic and photographic copying.

NATIONAL CASH REGISTER (NCR)
International branches
Microform readers. PCMI process for microfiche.
Trade microfilming.

OZALID
International branches or agents
Trade names: OZAFAX OZARAPID
Diazo. Photographic supplies. Small offset supplies.
Electrophotographic print out from microforms.

RICOH
Agents
Diazo. Electrophotographic copying. Small offset.

ROTAPRINT
Agents
Small offset.

VAN DER GRINTEN
International branches or agents
Diazo. Electrophotographic copying.

XEROX (XEROX CORPORATION IN USA: RANK-XEROX IN UK)
International branches
Electrophotographic copying.
A subsidiary is University Microfilms (Micropublishers and suppliers of
micro readers).

INDEX

Notes: 1 Organisations and manufacturers listed only in Chapter VIII are not indexed; 2 Books are indexed by author only; 3 A few entries are made under synonyms not used in the book (eg Gestetner).

Adherography 18
Adhesive (unsewn) binding 81
American Council of Learned
    Societies 43
Aperture cards 30, 31, 44, 68
Autopositive (direct positive)
    photocopying 55, 60, 61, 63

'Banda' (hectographic)
    duplicating 10, 12, 22, 26,
    65, 72-73, 78, 82
Bargain offers 17
Binding methods 79-82
Book copiers (flat bed) 13, 23,
    52, 56, 62, 64, 65
Books in English 46-47
British Library Lending Division
    43
British National Bibliography 46
Bulletin typewriters 94
Bureau (service) facilities 20,
    38, 39, 54, 68, 74, 78, 85

Camera methods in photo-
    copying 23, 53, 54, 55

Carbon copies 89
'CARD' microfiche system
    (Image System) 37, 43-44
Cartridges (microfilm) 30, 31, 39
Cassettes (microfilm) 30, 31, 39,
    46, 47
Catalogues 13, 46-47, 49, 72-
    73, 74-75
Centralised reprographic units
    15, 25, 73, 78-79
Chambers H T 100
Chemical (diffusion) transfer
    photocopying 19, 20, 55,
    59-60, 61, 62, 78
Ciné mode (microfilming) 28-
    30, 40
Coated paper (electrophoto-
    graphic) photocopying 67,
    68-69, 78
Coin operated machines 21, 69
Collating 79
Colour microfilm 27
Colour reproduction 11, 12, 18,
    22, 53-54, 72, 78, 84, 85
Coloured originals 23, 64, 65

COM (Computer Output Microfilm) 21, 38-39, 43, 46-47, 49
Comic mode (microfilming) 28-29
Consumer's Association 49
Contact photocopying 23, 53, 54, 55
Coordinates (microfiche) 40
Copyflo 44, 68
Copyright 14-15, 42
Costing 8, 18-21, 60-61
Covers of in-plant publications 84-85, 93-95
Crix, F C 98

De Bruin J H I 100
Design for in-plant work 75, 82-86
Design for microfilming 28-29, 39-40
Diazo microfiche duplicates 32-33
Diazo (dyeline) photocopying 22, 23, 54, 55, 59, 60, 62-63, 64, 71-72
Diazobond paper 63
Diffusion transfer photocopying 19, 20, 55, 59-60, 61, 62, 78
'Direct' exposure 23, 56-57, 62
Direct positive (autopositive) photocopying 55, 60, 61, 63
Display lettering 93-95
Double sided photocopying 69
Dual spectrum photocopying 55, 65
Duo microfilming 28
Duplex microfilming 28, 36
Duplicating (general) 10, 22, 24, 69

Dyeline (diazo) photocopying 22, 23, 54, 55, 59, 60, 62-63, 64, 71-72

Eichner (heat transfer) photocopying 55, 64-65, 72
Electric typewriters 88-89
Electrofax (zinc oxide) photocopying 67, 68-69, 78
Electrolytic process 36
Electronic stencil 65, 74
Electrophotographic (electrostatic) photocopying 9, 12, 13, 21, 23, 54, 55, 65-70, 78, 97
Encyclopedia Brittanica 44

Fee for copying 15
Filmorex 38, 43
Filmsetting 11, 82, 87, 92, 93, 94
Filmsort (aperture) cards 30, 31, 44, 68
Finding devices (microform readers) 37
Flat bed duplicators 72, 74
Flat bed photocopiers 13, 23, 52, 56, 62, 64, 65
Flow camera 36
Folding of printed sheets 79

Gardiner A W 98
Gelatin transfer photocopying 60
Gestetner (stencil) duplicating 10, 11, 64, 73-75, 77, 78, 82
'Golf ball' typewriters 90-91
Guardian newspaper 43

Hampshire T 8, 101
Harvester primary social sources
    45
Hatfield Polytechnic 8, 49
Hawken W R 99
Headings 84-85, 93-95
Heat transfer (Eichner)
    photocopying 55, 64-65, 72
Hectographic (spirit or Banda)
    duplicating 10, 12, 22, 26,
    65, 72-73, 78, 82

IBM 72 typewriters 90-91
Image Systems ('CARD' equip-
    ment) 37, 43-44
Information retrieval 30, 37-
    38, 43-44
'Instant print' shops 11, 12, 54
Institute of Reprographic
    Technology 15
Inter-library loans 43

Jacketed microfilm 30
Justification of text 11, 12, 83,
    89, 90, 91-93

Kalvar microfiche duplicates
    32-33

Layout for in-plant work 75,
    82-86
Layout for microfilming 28-29,
    39-40
Leisinger A H 99
Letraset 95
Letterpress printing 76, 77, 92,
    93, 95
Line selection (hectographic
    duplicating) 72-73

Linton W D 49
Lithographic printing (small
    offset) 10, 11, 22, 24, 75-79,
    82, 92
'Logo' device 85

Maintenance of machines 21
Manchester Guardian 43
Manchester public libraries 43
MARC tape cataloguing service
    46
Margins 82, 92
Mason D 14, 99
Mechanical (gelatin) transfer
    photocopying 60
Micro-litho 10, 33-34, 45-46
Micro-opaques 31, 33-34, 44
Microcard 33
Microfiche 30-33, 44
Microfiche duplicates 32-33, 34
Microfiche—stripping method
    32, 34
Microfilm Association of Great
    Britain 49
Microfilm processing 21, 25, 34
Microform print-outs 10, 11, 33,
    36-37, 48, 68
Microform readers 20, 28, 32,
    33, 35, 36, 37, 47-48
Micrographic Technology
    Corporation 37
Microprint 33, 34
Micropublishing 44-46
Mimeographing (stencil dupli
    cating) 10, 11, 64, 73-75,
    77, 78, 82
Miniaturised print 10, 33-34,
    45-46

Minicard 38, 43
Miracode 38
Multicopy transfer photo-
copying 18
Multilith (small offset) 10, 11,
22, 24, 75-79, 82, 92

National Cash Register 32, 46
National Reprographic Centre
for Documentation 8, 49
Negative microforms 32
Negative/positive photocopying
55, 59, 60-61
Non-camera photocopying 23,
53, 54, 55

Offset principle 76-77 *see also*
Small offset
Omnidex (microfilming) 40
Overhead projection transpar-
encies 64

PCMI fiche 12, 32, 44, 46-47
Package libraries in microform
44-45
Page S B 101
Pargeter P S 99
'Peel apart' (chemical transfer)
photocopying 19, 20, 55, 59-
60, 61, 62, 78
'Perfect' binding 81
Permanence 26, 51, 64, 65, 73
Photocharging 12, 13, 43
Photocomposition 11, 82, 87,
92, 93, 94
Photostabilisation 26, 59
Photostat 10, 25, 54-55, 67, 72
Planetary camera 34, 35
Plastic clip binding 81, 83
Plastic comb binding 81

Plate making (for small offset)
11, 60, 68, 69, 70, 75, 77-78
Plumb P W 49
Portable microform readers 36,
47-48
Proportional spacing 89, 90, 91
Purchase of equipment 17-18

Quality 11-13, 19, 21-22

Rapid selector 38, 43
Readex microprint 33, 44
Reduced size copies (photo-
copying and small offset)
69, 78, 83
Reduction ratios (microforms)
28, 32, 33, 39, 45, 46
Reel microfilm 27-31
Reflex exposure 57-58, 59, 60-
61, 62
'Reflex' photocopying 55, 59,
60-61
Rental facilities 21, 67, 69
Repro-typing 88-91, 92
Reprographic units 15, 25,
73, 78-79
Reversed reflex exposure 58-59,
60-61, 64
Rider, Freemont 41
Rockefeller Project 43
Roll feed photocopiers 69
Roneo (stencil) duplicating 10,
11, 64, 73-75, 77, 78, 82
Rotaprint (small offset) 10, 11,
22, 24, 75-79, 82, 92
Rotary photocopiers 13, 23,
53, 56, 62, 64

Saddle stitching 80-81
Selwyn R B 100

Service facilities 20, 38, 39, 54, 68, 74, 78, 86
'Shaded' faces (typewriter) 89
Silk screen printing 74
Silver halide microfiche duplicates 33
Silver halide photocopying 54, 55, 59-61
Simplex microfilming 28
Small offset 10, 11, 22, 24, 75-79, 82, 92
Sobey C 100
Speed of copying 24, 51
Spencer J R 98
Spiral binding 81
Spirit (hectographic) duplicating 10, 12, 22, 26, 65, 72-73, 78, 82
Stabbing (binding) 79-80, 83
Staffing 19, 25-26, 88
Standardisation in microforms 32, 47
Stapling 79-81
Stencil duplicating 10, 11, 64, 73-75, 77, 78, 82
Step and repeat camera 34
Superfiche 32

Tape typewriters 93
Thermofax photocopying 22, 26, 55, 64, 74
Thermographic (heat) photocopying 12, 23, 54, 55, 63-65
Tone illustrations 11, 12, 22, 53, 59, 68, 69, 75, 77, 87
Total copy (automatic duplicating) systems 77

Type faces 84, 85
Typewriter composition 91-93
Typewriter faces—interchangeable 89-91
Typewriter ribbons 89
Typewriters 82, 87-92

Ultrafiche 12, 32, 44, 46-47
Unitised microfilm 30
University Microfilms 68, 100
Unsewn binding 81
User resistance to microforms 37, 41, 46, 48, 49-50

Varitypers 90-91, 93
Verifax 60
Verry H R 101
Vesicular microfiche duplicates 32-33

'Walnut' information retrieval system 38, 43, 44
Wastage 12, 19, 26, 34, 60, 95
Wax stencil duplicating 10, 11, 64, 73-75, 77, 78, 82
Williams B J S 8, 14, 98, 99
Wright G H 49, 101

Xerox duplication 70, 71, 78, 79
Xerox photocopying (xerography) 67-70 see also Electrophotographic photocopying

Zinc oxide (Electrofax) photocopying 67, 68-69, 78